Listening to Old Pete

Listening to Old Pete

A HISTORIC ALTERNATIVE

Robert W. Taylor

VANTAGE PRESS
New York

Copyright © 2000 by Robert W. Taylor

Published by Vantage Press, Inc.
516 West 34th Street, New York, New York 10001

Manufactured in the United States of America
ISBN: 0-533-13056-5

Library of Congress Catalog Card No.: 98-91117

0 9 8 7 6 5 4 3 2 1

Prologue

Nineteen ninety-eight marks the one hundred and thirty-fifth commemoration of the bloodiest battle on the North American continent—the Battle of Gettysburg. With the dawn of a new millennium a scant two years away, this year affords the twentieth-century historian his best rationale for pausing one more time to analyze the "Turning Point" of his nation's most costly conflict before "crossing over the river" with his contemporaries into the uncertain future. "Uncertain" because new dawns tend to have their own special dichotomy—they can illuminate the path we are on or momentarily blind us if we look directly at them. Further, whether we take a "bridge" into the new millennium (as our current president suggests) or a Ford (as the men of '63 more often did than not), it is good to keep in our collective pack what has proven valuable in getting us to this point.

One of the valuable constants in the American experience across the three centuries referred to above; is our belief that human life is the supreme measure of all that is valuable—what Lincoln termed "the last full measure of devotion" as he stood before Cemetery Hill. To point out, as I did above, that Gettysburg and the war of which it was the turning point was the "most costly" is to say that what was purchased should have the greatest value to us as a nation. In his attempt to avoid what some call our "irrepressible conflict," Daniel Webster sought to fuse

"Liberty and Union" as "one and inseparable," but they were separate entities pulling apart the very heart of our national character, and 600,000 lives were spent on the valuable lesson that only a strong UNION could insure LIBERTY for its citizenry.

To the defeated Southerner, of course, such might did not make the primacy of UNION over LIBERTY "right," and yet, proof that it did existed in his own oxymoronic strategy of waging a War for Independence based on local (states') RIGHTS. Next to the armies of the UNION, therefore, the Southern emphasis on parochial independence proved to be its own worst enemy. A glaring example of this occurred when Governor Brown of Georgia, "the rebel's rebel," kept more troops at home to guard localities under the golden aegis of "state sovereignty" than he was willing to devote to the common cause of stopping Sherman's March to the Sea.

Today, as we approach the bridges and Fords to the new millennium, the greatest threat to American UNITY no longer comes from the doctrine of state's rights. Indeed, the last Republican presidential candidate of this century proudly exhibited the Tenth Amendment that he carried over his heart throughout the campaign. Nonetheless, the greatest threat to our shared American experience at this time results from a gradual "leeching" downward of the state's rights doctrine via the "ME" generation of the 1980s into the multifaceted agendas of the so-called "special interest groups" of the 1990s. "It is NOT OUR BUSINESS," Senator Barbara Boxer proclaimed on May 20, 1997 when the American Congress was asked to reconcile the irreconcilable fault line created by the acrimonious positions of "PRO-LIFE" versus "PRO-CHOICE" groups over partial-birth abortions.

To halt the divisiveness of such "special interest

1860

A HOUSE DIVIDED

groups" now assailing our nation's capital more forcefully than Lee's legions, we must promote a conviction that it is "NOT THE BUSINESS" of public policy to accurately reflect or promote the multifarious prejudices of individuals masquerading under the multicolored banners of "special interest groups." "A house divided CANNOT stand" was one of the valuable lessons we should have learned 135 years ago when the lesson-giver saw only three issues splitting Northern and Southern "interests," i.e., (PRO/ANTI-*Slavery*; LOW/HIGH *Tariffs*; STATE'S/ POPULAR *Rights*). Today, these few issues pale in comparison to the innumerable issues raised by special interest groups most of whom are clamoring for the "RIGHT" to inject their agenda into NATIONAL policy. (See 1990s prototype for an 1864 cartoon.)

It is the hope of the author that in *Listening to Old Pete* we can discover some hidden lesson within his "Historic Alternative" that might be worthwhile to recall as we commemorate the one hundred and thirty-fifth turning point of the great American epic known as the Civil War. My method for such a discovery was designed to avoid the largely irrelevant ruminations of the "Monday morning quarterback" whose "what ifs" simply transpose twentieth-century alternatives back into the record of our most divisive conflict. Rather, my analysis will be of two actual alternatives posed in 1863 by a primary actor in that conflict, James Longstreet.

There are both personal and collective benefits for us today in "Listening to Old Pete." Personally, like many of us today, Longstreet considered himself the equal of those whom society had designated his "superiors." Having recognized this fact, it probably goes without saying that Longstreet was deeply disappointed by Lee's rejection of his Gettysburg "alternative" in July 1863 and

Bragg's rejection of his Chattanooga "alternative" two months later. After the war, the longest-serving corps commander of an army, "conceived and dedicated" to the cause of State's Rights, joined the party that had "saved the Union" and penned his autobiography while serving variously as American minister to Turkey, United States Marshal, and United States Commissioner of Railroads. In so doing, Longstreet lived out Webster's revelation shortly before the latter's death in 1852:

The UNION is United, Not Consolidated
NOT Chaos-like together, crushed and bruised
But, like the world, harmoniously CONFUSED
Where ORDER in Variety we see and
Where though all things differ,
All Agree!

Part I

One

If I had taken General Longstreet's advice on the eve of the second day of the Battle of Gettysburg, and filed off the left corps of my army behind the right corps, in the direction of Washington and Baltimore, along the Emmittsburg Road, the Confederates would today be a free people.
R. E. Lee in *Eclectic Magazine*, 5/72

Since the objective of " . . . A Historic Alternative" is to determine the consequences of "Listening to Old Pete" in 1863, we too must eventually file off "along the Emmitsburg Road in the direction of Washington and Baltimore." Whether this road would have led to the purely political objective of Southern Independence, however, is a determination that lies outside the scope of this narrative. Longstreet's suggestion that the Army of Northern Virginia should move around the left flank of the Army of the Potomac at Gettysburg—just as he suggested the Army of Tennessee do against Rosecrans two months later—was a tactical one and our focus will be on analyzing how such a tactic would have altered the military record of our Civil War one hundred and thirty-five years ago.

It is an irony within the historical record that the Commander of the Union army at Gettysburg, George Gordon Meade, predicted an attack on his center the night before Longstreet was ordered to make it.[1] Using the process of elimination, Meade had detained John Gibbon at the close of the Council of War held on the night of July 2nd to observe: "General Gibbon, if Lee attacks tomorrow, it will be on your front." When Gibbon questioned this conclusion, Meade pointed out that it was the only part of the Union line yet to be attacked by the Confederates. According to Douglas Southall Freeman, Longstreet was still developing his plan for enveloping the Union left on Little Round Top when Lee approached First Corps Headquarters at dawn, July 3rd, with definitive orders to attack the Union center.[2] The record of Longstreet's opposition to Pickett's Charge, however, began long before Meade's fortuitous (for him) prediction.

Before the Army of Northern Virginia even crossed the Potomac, the "dispersed defensive" strategy it had successfully employed during the "Peninsula Campaign", Manassas, Fredericksburg and Chancellorsville, had been defined by the political objective of achieving (maintaining?) Southern Independence.[3] Although it was not immediately relevant to such an objective that the North be invaded and conquered by offensive action, an affirmative conclusion had not been reached without its share of debate both in and outside the Confederate capital at Richmond. If Thomas Paine had noted during America's first War for Independence, "We win by a DRAWN game," there seldom was unanimity among the "colonels" in and out of the Confederate Congress as to where the lines for that "game" should be drawn. With this in mind, it was perhaps only "natural" that a debate over strategic objectives and the tactics needed to achieve those objectives would accompany the Southern Army as it moved north into Pennsylvania in mid-1863.

Thus, when "Old Pete" first observed the Union position on Cemetery Ridge through his field glasses shortly after five P.M. on July 1st, he was actually heartened that the ridge's rough sides and uneven terrain would retard Federal assaults against the Southern line being arrayed along Seminary Ridge. Here would be another Fredericksburg, the ideal Confederate battle, in which Northern assaults against defensive positions could be repulsed with little cost and great consequences. Turning to Lee, Longstreet observed, "We could not call the enemy to position better suited to our plans. All that we have to do is to file around his left and secure good ground between him and his capital."[4]

Thinking his commanding officer in complete accord with this assessment of both the strategic objective of the northern incursion and the tactical maneuver needed to accomplish it vis-à-vis the Union position on Cemetery Ridge, Longstreet was "a little surprised" when Lee emphatically proclaimed, "If he is there tomorrow, I will attack him."[5]

It would become apparent in subsequent years that much of Longstreet's immediate surprise and the misunderstandings surrounding Pickett's Charge (i.e., an ASCENT of Cemetery Ridge) two days later grew out of a difference between Lee and him on the difference between "intentions" and "pledges."

In 1868, Lee mentioned "a reported correspondence with Longstreet," in which the latter referred to a pledge Lee had made to avoid a general battle in Pennsylvania. Lee, for his part, thought "that this idea was absurd, that he never made any such promise and never thought of . . . any such thing." Always the gentleman, hesitant to attack his "old war horse," Lee mused in 1868 that probably Longstreet had never made such a statement about his commander's intentions before leaving Virginia.[6] Yet, in his official account of the Gettysburg campaign, Lee reported,

> It had not been intended to deliver a general battle so far from our base unless attacked. But coming unexpectedly upon the whole Federal Army, to withdraw through the mountains with our extensive trains would have been difficult and dangerous.

Ironically, not even the unmovable mountains were immune from the debate over tactics since Lee had observed to General Anderson five hours before conferring with Longstreet on Seminary Ridge, " . . . if we do not gain a victory, those defiles and gorges which we passed this morning will shelter us from disaster."[7]

Another cautionary against a frontal attack at Gettysburg lies in the "bible" of Civil War tactics used by both North and South. General Hardee's *Tactics* emphasized envelopment of the enemy's flank (right or left) as the key to victory on the battlefield. Bases of fire and, indeed, "fire superiority" could be established by the center, but frontal assaults were not a highly recommended tactic in this manual. Thus it was that Longstreet's greatest display of frustration at Gettysburg was registered not against Lee or the "doomed" Pickett, who enthusiastically moved out against the Union center on July 3rd, but against John B. Hood for pointing out to him the painfully obvious on July 2nd, i.e.,—that by moving around the Union's flank on Little Round top, their left could be turned, its supply trains captured and an interposition gained between the Army of the Potomac and its capital.[8]

It is probably appropriate at this time in " . . . A Historic Alternative" to ask what additional evidence exists in the historical record that Lee would be more receptive to the tactical suggestions of his First Corps Commander by July 3rd. The record shows that on June 29th, when Ewell's Second Corps reached the northernmost thrust of the Southern Army ten miles from Harrisburg, Lee issued orders that it return to Cashtown twenty-five miles to the south to assume a defensive position and "await attack" with the rest of the army. It was A. P. Hill's instruction to cover this defensive concentration at Cashtown that "by chance" placed his ill-shod corps near the town of Gettysburg. The "rest is History," for as Morrison and Commager note in their *Growth of the American Republic,* "Hill's zeal for footwear changed the battle from a defensive one near Cashtown to an offensive one at Gettysburg."[9] It is safe to assume from this observation that Lee (like Meade) had not completely abandoned his preference for a defensive engagement to "chance."

A second factor in explaining Lee's receptivity to an alternate tactic on July 3rd was the report of his headquarters engineer, Captain S. R. Johnston. Johnston (along with Major Clarke of Longstreet's staff) had been sent by Lee to reconnoitre the Union left early on July 2nd. Johnston's report, eagerly awaited by Lee, was finally delivered around six A.M. when the latter was in conference with Longstreet and A. P. Hill on Seminary Ridge. Johnston assured Lee he had used an "eminence" on Little Round Top to observe that there were no organized Union forces in that sector. A ride south of Little Round Top had encountered only three or four cavalrymen galloping north toward Gettysburg.[10] Although Lee actually used this report to support his plan for an oblique attack by Longstreet against Cemetery Ridge, the seed was nonetheless planted in his mind that turning the Union left was "doable."

A third factor in the historical record, which would

explain Lee's propensity for "Listening to Old Pete" on July 3rd would be the sudden arrival of his "eyes and ears" in the form of Stuart's Calvary on the afternoon of July 2nd. Although much speculation exists about the actual exchange between the two men, two factors exist indelibly in the record: 1. Stuart's route to Gettysburg had taken him through Union Mills, Maryland, which was the heart of Meade's proposed defensive line at Pipe Creek. 2. Stuart would vigorously defend this route and his actions along it as being of value to the Army of Northern Virginia. Receiving Stuart's report, which will be examined in greater detail later, the now-composed Lee concluded, "You must now help me fight these people." It is doubtful that having said this, Lee would then relegate Stuart's 5,000 men to a passive role on the Confederate left.

That part of the historical record presented above sets a primary stage for, at least, *Lee's consideration* of an alternative to Pickett's Charge as he dismounted at First Corps Headquarters at dawn, July 3rd. Further, according to the record, Longstreet wasted no time in urging such an alternative as he now stepped forward to greet his commanding officer: "General, I have had my scouts out all night, and I find that you still have an excellent opportunity to move around the right of Meade's army and maneuver him into attacking us."

When Lee bluntly confirmed his plan to attack the Union center with a massed attack by the entire First Corps, Longstreet asserted the impossibility of such an attack based on the events of the previous day. Both McLaws and Hood he explained, were now "cheek and jowl" with the enemy on Little Round Top and any attempt to withdraw their divisions for the purpose of supporting Pickett at the center would expose them to a murderous enfilade that would crumble the Confederate right flank.

At this point in the historical record, Lee begins "Listening to Old Pete," for he responds, " . . . take Pickett's division and make the attack. I will reinforce you by two divisions of the Third Corps"—Heth's and half of Pender's.[11] Certainly this concession to one of Longstreet's major criticisms of a frontal assault would serve to hearten him. Unfortunately for the South, however, this concession remains in the historical record as a major reason for the failure of Pickett's Charge, for as Douglas Southall Freeman notes in *Lee's Lieutenants:* "This decision to use Heth appears to have been made quickly and without ascertaining the condition of the troops. The omission was to prove itself one of the worst of the many mistakes of Gettysburg." Yet, when one applies the certainty of Longstreet's renewed confidence to Lee's obvious haste to remedy his objections, the omission Freeman refers to disappears from our "Historical Alternative": i.e.,

> Longstreet: "Has any determination been made as to the condition of Heth's division?"
> Lee: "No, but I will direct Colonel Venable to make such a determination and report back to us as soon as practicable."

Colonel Venable, of Lee's Headquarter's staff, would recall after the war that lacking such a report, "they were terribly mistaken about Heth's division in this planning." It had NOT recuperated, having suffered more than was reported on the first day. Here then is where the historical record and our "historical alternative" coincide, for

such a report delivered to Lee and Longstreet in the early
morning of July 3, 1863 would read:

Headquarters,
Third Corps
Army of Northern Virginia

General Lee,

General Heth remains disabled from his head wound
and Pettigrew has assumed command of the division.

Of the six brigades available to support Pickett, only
Lane's is commanded by a brigadier of tested combat experience.

Both Archer's and Davis's Brigades are almost without field officers with many regiments currently being directed by company officers.

If these units are to comprise two-thirds of the attacking column, should they not remain under Third
Corps command?

Respectfully, A.P. Hill
Lieutenant General, Commanding

Lee would most likely fold this report pensively and
look toward Longstreet: "General, let us look at your plan
for enveloping General Meade's left."

Two

General, I have been in combat with men in squads, companies, brigades, divisions and corps. There is no way 15,000 men so arrayed can take that position.
—Longstreet to Lee on Pickett's Charge 7/3/63

My name is Jeremiah Gere, presently serving in the Army of Northern Virginia, Hill's Corps, Heth's Division, Fourth Brigade, Eleventh Mississippi Regiment, Company A (University Grays). I am identified in the historical record as the first Southern casualty of Pickett's Charge on July 3, 1863, since an old hip wound kept me from hugging the ground during the Federal reply to Colonel Alexander's cannonade preceding the attack.[1] I'll leave the details of my demise, however, to Dr. Holt, assistant surgeon of the Eleventh Mississippi, since this "historic alternative" to the historic record grants me both new liberty and responsibility. Now that General Lee is "Listening to Old Pete," I was given a few extra days (months or years?) to tell you about the roads taken before and after what history records as both the fateful day for my life and the Cause of Southern Independence.

I was born in 1838 to my parents, John and Lydia Gere, in our family's Georgian-revival homestead situated five miles east of Vicksburg, Mississippi. My father, who had inherited two dilapidated river packets about the same time he inherited me, had commenced a modest shipping business between Vicksburg and Cincinnati, Ohio. Mother, meanwhile, spent my early years educating me in the British classics, which she seemingly loved with a different intensity than that reserved for Father and me. In addition, Mother served a more practical role in supervising our house and storage facilities when Father was down at the docks or "upriver" on business. Whether for reasons of economy or morality, our family never "employed" or used slave labor and I can not remember any workers—white or free black—complaining he hadn't been paid fair and on time. On my tenth birthday, my parents' roles converged through my invitation to accompany Father to Cincinnati along with a small book of Blake's poems presented to me by Mother earlier that day.

Cincinnati was the first big city I had ever seen and it seemed to surround and engulf me. Vicksburg, you see, sits on a high bluff overlooking the "Father of Waters." At this place, one's view is first drawn westward over these magnificent natural wonders toward the great expanses newly won from Mexico. To my young imagination, therefore, Vicksburg seemed to be simply a man-made platform designed solely for the viewing of our Creator's natural and historic powers—the one flowing majestically southward beneath my feet and the other rolling westward in the "Manifest Destiny" of our nation to reach the Pacific Ocean. The co-joining of such powers was breathtaking no matter how often I gazed upon them.

In Cincinnati, I felt choked. The endless monotony of street "grids," the omnipresent stench of slaughterhouse and smokestack accompanied by the ceaseless clanging of manufactures threw such a pall of melancholia over me that earlier images of Hades described in Sunday School took definitive shape for the first time in my young life.

When Father was late for supper on our last night, I took
to reading my book on Blake's poetry for escape and stum-
bled on another person who seemingly shared my feelings
about the city in his poem about London. For diversion, I
engaged in a little plagiarism, which simply involved sub-
stituting the Ohio River for Blake's Thames. If memory
serves after fifteen years—there goes General Hill to confer with Lee and Longstreet—I'll recite the deed below:

Cincinnati
**(*revised by J. Gere from Blake's "London" at
age 10, 1848*)**

I wander through each chartered street
Near where the chartered Ohio flows and
Mark in every face I meet
Marks of weakness, marks of woe.

In every voice, in every van
In every infant's cry of fear
In every curse and every ban
The mind-forged manacles I hear.

How the chimney-sweeper's cry,
Every blackening church appals and
How the hapless tenant's sigh
Runs in Blood down airless Halls.

But most through mid-night streets I hear
How the youthful harlot's curse
Blasts the new-born Infant's tear and
Blights with plagues the Marriage hearse.

We were halfway down the Ohio River the next day before I worked up the courage to tell Father how my reaction to Cincinnati "allowed me" to plagiarize William Blake. I remember being pleasantly surprised by his reaction. "You're turning into a regular Jeffersonian, son," he quipped. Father then launched into a little lecture on how the author of our Declaration of Independence (and founder of the Democratic Party to which Father belonged) had also distrusted cities. It seems that in establishing the University of Virginia, Jefferson even left open, like the "natural" design of Vicksburg, the western view near his home to reflect his hope that our new Republic would retain its agrarian base.

My father was a businessman and never developed the habit, as did Mother, of quoting authors to his son, so that is why I remember vividly what he said as our packet reached the confluence of the Ohio and Mississippi. We had walked over to the starboard side to view the setting sun, and Father, grasping the railing with such intensity his knuckles went white, recited from some boyhood lesson the words of his favorite statesman as the Illinois shore receded in the gathering twilight off our stern: "When we get piled on top of one another in cities like they are in Europe, we will begin to eat one another as they do there." I'll admit to a vast relief that Father had chosen to compare my feelings to his favorite political hero, rather than my cheating words to Mother's favorite British author! I turned in and slept soundly rocked gently by the currents bearing me home from my first Northern adventure.

As it turned out, the most heated discussion waiting for us back home involved a story in one of the Cincinnati newspapers that my father usually brought back for

Mother after his trips "up river." This story involved a Women's Rights Convention, or some such, that had been held at Seneca Falls, New York, the week before my tenth birthday. Mother began urging Father to "fish or cut bait" on the attempt of these women to apply Jefferson's Declaration to themselves. Entitled the "Declaration of Sentiments," their document proclaimed, "All Men AND Women are created Equal," regarding the rights and responsibilities of citizenship.

The most vivid recollection I have of my parents' ensuing debate (since I wasn't much for reading newspapers at this age) involves a pen and ink drawing of a Miss Amelia Bloomer on the front page of the paper in question. This woman had developed pants (or pantaloons) for women with the idea men and women should also dress alike if they were to be so treated in the future. Once during this parental debate, when Father seemed to be at a loss for words, the little devil in me handed Miss Bloomer's picture over to him.

"That's right," he said glancing down at my contribution, "if men and women looked and acted the same, what reason would I have for marrying the latter? The good thing about men and women according to both the Good Book and Newton, is that opposites attract and provide a balance for one another. Night has day, summer has winter, and gender differences are part of that natural scheme, Proclamations and Declarations not withstanding!" Initially, I felt a little guilty for tilting the so-called "balance" of the debate against Mother, two-to-one, but that feeling vanished somewhat when I noticed Father wink good-naturedly in her direction. Fully eight years would pass before I realized this signaled me as the odd man out of the first gender-equality debate in my young life.

Just before I left for college, I learned Father had provided that most of his estate, with the exception of the two packets aforementioned, would be left to Mother. In his realm of Southern society, where entail and primogeniture were still unofficially practiced, it had been appropriate (easy/expedient) for him to espouse in public places the intention to paint "and SON" after his name on those two packets. Despite actually doing this, John Gere's son had grown to manhood knowing that Mother was both John Gere's lifetime and business partner. What I realized on the eve of my departure for college, was that Father's *gentlemanliness* had not only broken loose the parochial restrictions of his Southern culture, but had transcended the best vision of those social reformers who had gathered at Seneca Falls. To John Gere, it seems now to me, people were people first and the fact that they were born black or female was of secondary importance. Just as he never told me that the statesman he admired most had drawn a line against the spread of the wealthy slave-owners above the Ohio, so he never told me that the love he felt for Mother had marked an indelible boundary against the male-dominant attitudes of the "meaner sort" with whom he also had daily contact. To this day, some inverse social proposition makes it easier for me to "hob-nob" with people I least admire. Perhaps the Lucretia Motts and William Garrisons of our day should heed the warning of that old philosopher, "Be careful of what you wish for . . . "

An aide to General Hill just returned to Third Corps Headquarters and the rumor floating back to our Grays is that "Old Pete" wants to disengage from this tussle and move around the Yankees toward Washington or Baltimore. He figures Meade would have no choice but to pull off those heights in front and try to beat us to his capital.

Sounds like a good plan to me since it wouldn't cost as much as a frontal attack and we travel lighter and faster than Billy, but then, I'm no officer, so who knows? On with my story—

In 1855, my family agreed I would attend the University of Mississippi at Oxford with a major in literature when I turned eighteen. Those four years were the most influential ones in my life and, as it turned out, the life of our Nation. Each year as I pursued my studies, it seemed events were spinning the clock faster and faster toward a sectional conflict. In November 1856, just two months after I arrived at Oxford, the new Republican Party put up John Fremont as its first presidential candidate. Father claimed that radical Abolitionists and northern businessmen were using "The Pathfinder" to mask their platform of Free Soil, High Tariffs, and a Nationalized Banking System. If so, their plan failed when James Buchanan was elected with his conviction that the Supreme Court should settle the slavery issue since, as our most stable branch of government, it had not been subject to campaign pandering and stood closest to the Constitution.

Of course, there was a big problem in getting closer to the Constitution—more heat than light was generated more often than not. In fact, I would designate getting closer to the Constitution as one of the root causes of this sectional conflict. From the days of Thomas Jefferson to those of John Calhoun, we Southerners had viewed this document as a creation of the states. Born in 1776 with the Declaration of Independence, the states were invited eleven years later by their Confederation Congress to simply "revise the Articles of Confederation." Under the doctrine of natural law espoused by Jefferson, it was impossible for us to conceive that what was created had more power than its creators. The resulting compact for the whole could NOT be greater than the sum of its parts. Like an elder parent to its younger child, the states "naturally" retained the power to nullify any act, which showed the Federal government was getting too big for its britches. Maybe secession is just nullification of those planks kept in the platform of the Republican Party that the Supreme Court had declared unconstitutional back in 1857.

Northerners, meanwhile, had taken a narrower view of the Constitution, which was based solely on its first three words—"We the People." This so-called "national" view of our Union was conceived by the political enemies of Jefferson, nurtured by National Bank agents like Dan Webster and handed over to Abe Lincoln. This view is based on the Might (not Right) of the "numerical majority" that claims when three out of four "people" want a higher tariff on imports, for example, there is nothing the fourth citizen can do but surrender his liberty and march in lockstep with the majority then in fashion. The blatant hypocrisy of this theory was shown time and again by Lincoln in 1858 and 1860, but at this point, dear reader, you must be wondering how a literature major like myself got so interested in law and politics. Well, after I started my senior year at Ole Miss in 1859, it seemed that, unlike the country, the two fields had become one. You couldn't pick up a magazine, newspaper or tome without running into the political differences I outlined above. Whether it was for this reason or my meeting of Billy Lowry, I remained at Oxford after graduation to enter the law school in the fall of 1860.[2]

Previous to my temporary conversion to the law, Lincoln, who had been prattling Webster that the Constitution was made "by the people, for the people and answerable to the people" had been beaten by Douglas running for the Senate seat chosen by the STATE Legislature of Illinois!

Of course, the "people" didn't have anything to do with this election unless you want to make the flip-flop of calling the Illinois legislature at Springfield, "the people." Now, if you were able to pull off this flip-flop, you're ready for the one Old Abe pulled in November 1860. Most of "the people" in this Presidential Election (2,231,069) voted for the Democratic party candidates (Douglas's 1,382,713 people; Breckenridge's 848,356 people) to Abe's 1,865,593 "people." When the Republican Party nullified the "people's will" by counting instead each *State's* strength in Congress (electoral college), most of our folks just "nullified" Old Abe and the Republicans. As the *Oxford Mercury* for November 21, 1860 observed:

> The Union was founded for the common safety and protection for all the states. Now it is on the eve of passing into the hands of Abraham Lincoln, a coarse, illiterate, low-born scoundrel . . . who intends to pervert it for the oppression and annihilation of the South.

Well, that's one Southerner's view of how this fight came about, and I'm sure that in a War for Southern Independence, there is plenty of room for others, but it was about this time that I met Billy Lowry.

Dear Reader, if you thought my views on states' rights sounded too parochial, you should have met Billy Lowry when I did. In our army, it's easy to tell where a man's heart lies when you meet them in outfits designated the Fifteenth "Alabama" or "The Richmond Howitzers," but Billy loved those lovely manicured lawns of our campus at Oxford so much, he continued to embrace them even when he was expelled for missing too many classes.

You see, when most of us were carrying books, pencils and rules to class, Billy was galloping over the grounds with bird gun in hand with his dog and slave close behind in that order. It was in the person of Billy that my love of the Southern landscape and my distaste for Northern hypocrisy co-joined when he called us to form the Company of University Grays in December 1860.

Fixed in my memory for all time will be the sights, sounds and smells of the following spring at Oxford when we "University soldiers" marched and drilled amidst magnolia-lined fields as our pulchitrudinous admirers, attired in every color of the rainbow, waved and applauded softly with white-gloved hands. I guess others admired our uniforms of gray, trimmed in red and topped off with black hats as well because when President Davis called for volunteers after Sumter, forty-two of our seventy-nine member company was comprised of non-students from the town—clerks, mechanics and some farmboys.[3]

At five A.M. on May 1, 1861, Father arrived at our departure ceremony just as the faculty farewells were being presented. Mother had stayed at home as was usual to conduct business in his stead although Father indicated to me that she held more private reasons for being absent this particular time. Nonetheless, my ability to record these reminiscences for you was made possible by her parting gift of a handsome leather and brass-bound writing pad. As Father stood to the right of our company that spring morning, it appears we both noticed how anxiously Dr. Ballard, Chancellor of the University, scanned the now nearly-deserted campus. I'm glad Billy didn't hear what he said next since it sure would have removed a lot of starch from his collar: "My college seems to be the first casualty of the war."[4] Billy, I guess you already figured, felt we were fighting for and not against the University. Well, since the time we elected Billy the Company Commander, he's been kicked so far up the ranks, I rarely get to see him anymore. How's that for combining a grassroots choice of "the people" with the innate ability of an individual to rise to the top of the creamer?

Now that General Hill has returned, the rumor mill is working overtime. It seems the disengagement is planned to start from the Confederate left to right with Dick Ewell's Second Corps pulling off Culp's and Cemetery Hill through Gettysburg and down our rear here on Seminary Ridge. Once clear of our line, we are to follow Second Corps down to the Emmittesburg Road. Compared to our other two corps, about a mile separates us from the Yankees, so we should have the easiest time of it. As a matter of fact, some of us were just joking that we could be in Washington before the Yankees in our front knew we were gone. Lastly, Old Pete wants to extricate his divisions on Round Top under a massed cannonade. Apparently his artillery chief, Colonel Alexander, plans to borrow some of our guns because I heard one of our artillerists complain First Corps already had enough to knock fifty feet off Little Round Top. We'll see what we will see. Right now, with your indulgence, I'd like to get back to the cream that rises naturally without the benefit of "bullets or ballots," Parrots or Proclamations.

Six months ago, on January 1, 1863, Abe and his Abolitionist friends tried to make elevating slaves as the second major objective of this war. Of course, the way it was worded, the so-called Emancipation Proclamation didn't free a single slave, but it sure gave those Northern hypocrites an excellent fall-back position after what they did two weeks ago on June 19th. After denouncing secession as unconstitutional and a threat to the Union for two years, they just up and annexed several counties in Virginia, which wanted out of the Old Dominion, as the Northern "free" state of West Virginia! I reckon their Constitutional principles against forming states out of existing ones didn't bother these "Unionists." At any rate, slaves living in this new state are probably untouched by Abe's Proclamation because their owners are no longer "in rebellion" against the Union (more "flip-flops")!

Well, I guess you can tell by now that your narrator isn't much in favor of proclamations or bullets as a desirable democratic method of removing vertical distinctions in nature or society. It stands to reason that if the North is seeking to elevate the blacks by this method, they are seeking to de-elevate the planter class, which is based on slavery. I believe, however, that once the thrust of any Republican government is aimed at removing vertical distinctions in favor of a leveling equalitarianism, it dooms itself to the frustrations of continual failure for two reasons: 1. Individuals, by definition, are different and some (like Billy Lowry) will "naturally" rise or stand out from others in the various fields of human endeavor. 2. The failure to recognize #1 through Acts and Proclamations aimed at making everyone "equal" (or the same) is characteristic of undemocratic governments, which view attempts to assert one's uniqueness as destructive to social order.

Now just in case you think the above comments represent the ravings of a Southern bigot, I remind you that my "middling class" family prospered despite its covert opposition to slave labor and secondly that my literary studies brought me into contact with many enlightened writers in America and Europe, including the most popular American author in Europe today, Mr. James Fenimore Cooper.[5]

In *The American Democrat* (1838), which I encountered during my third year at Oxford, Cooper explodes the notion that social equality should be the aim of democratic governments. "Some men," he wrote

> fancy that a democrat can only be one who seeks the level social, mental and morals of the majority, a rule that at once would exclude all men of refinement, education and taste from the class. These persons are ENEMIES of DEMOCRACY, as they at once render it impracticable.

The way I see it, Cooper believed democracy only required that each citizen have one vote in the government. Any subsequent attempt by that government, however, to remove vertical distinctions in society in favor of some undifferentiated mass, is as inimical to a free society as the reign of terror was to the original precepts of the French Revolution. Enter the American Robespierre, Lincoln whose Radical friends talk of confiscating plantations and turning them over to the Freedmen. Cooper went on to point out,

> Manners, education and refinement are productive of high enjoyments; and it is as unjust to deny their possessors their indulgence as it would be to insist on the less fortunate's passing the time they would rather devote to athletic amusements, in listening to opera for which they have no relish, sung in a language they do not understand.[6]

The Lincoln government, of course, is playing for meaner stakes than just emancipating the blacks from slavery. They plan to win black support for the Republican Party long after this war is over. You can already see in some Northern editorials we picked up this side of the

Potomac that they are planning to tag themselves the party of UNION and FREEDOM next year while the Democrats will be painted as the party of SECESSION and SLAVERY. Well, I never did place stock in political labeling strategy since, like Father, I view people as individuals first rather than just members of a particular race or gender. The Republicans can no more bank on ALL BLACKS supporting their party any more than those women at Seneca Falls back in '48 could bank on ALL WOMEN supporting their platform. No matter who wins this war, change is going to be the only constant and if the Democratic Party goes down as a result, we rebs just might have no other choice than to infiltrate the party left standing.

I see the boys are packing up now and Doctor Holt is even calling for volunteers to break down the field hospital. I've rambled on enough to you, so I'll see if I can be of any assistance to him. "Hallo, Sir! No harvest of arms or legs today?"

"No, Corporal, not today, but Meade will not let us slip away to Washington without a contest. I'll help you with that canvas as soon as I consign these papers to the flames."

After throwing several duplicate copies of regimental sick calls and casualty lists into the dying embers of the breakfast fire, Dr. Holt withdrew a partially-finished letter to his wife from a breast pocket. Like the medical reports of a Confederate regiment poised on Seminary Ridge, July 3, 1863, this letter too was part of the historical record consigned to the flames on that day. With this, the historical alternative to Pickett's Charge begins to unfold with the sun climbing higher over Cemetery Ridge and the grove of trees that today's visitor knows as the "High Water Mark of the Confederacy." Like Dr. Holt, therefore, we too take a passing glance at his Sally's letter before following the University Grays down the shaded lane behind Seminary Ridge toward a different destination.

Gettysburg, July 3, 1863

My Dearest Sally,

Today our army conducted a frontal assault against the Yankees ensconced on fortified ridges south of the small college town of Gettysburg. It was both a fearful and magnificent maneuver to behold and was preceded by a cannonade the likes of which this continent has never beheld. I sometimes believe, however, that the soldier in the ranks can easier escape the heartbreak attending the instantaneous death or maiming of his comrades by averting his glance to right or left and fixing it on the valuable prize ahead. As a surgeon charged with saving those lives, however, it seems all the agony and heartbreak is brought back to my feet with such unrealistic hope in the eyes of attendants and wounded of a recovery and resurrection so far beyond my poor skills, that my spirit is habitually sunk into a despair mere words can not describe. It is my confirmed belief that on July 3rd I would have succumbed to this despair and quit the ranks as surgeon if it were not for a perceived miracle attending our first casualty. I beg your indulgence, dear Sally, for the rest of this letter is devoted to the miracle of Jeremiah.

This youth in his mid-twenties, was brought to me at the onset of the artillery exchange. His large frame, covered with a gray blanket, overlapped the stretcher by a half foot and was topped by a head of golden hair, which framed such unusual blue eyes, that they at once riveted me by their combination of brightness and calm. The calm I first attributed to the superficial wound in his left arm, which hung limply out from the blanket, for I remember

25

telling him it could be saved with minor surgery. "No, Doctor," he said, "this is where I was hit," throwing back the blanket with his other arm to reveal the most horrific wound I had ever witnessed. I remember briefly growing faint, but those riveting eyes held me upright. The entire front part of his torso from hip to rib cage had been torn laterally from his body by shrapnel, exposing areas of the anatomy I have only seen on those corpses we dissected in medical training. How his heart continued beating and his mind clear can only be answered in realms beyond this world. His request of me to make his end less painful seemed natural enough, however, and I poured a cup of black drop for his immediate consumption, asking with half-numbed recitation if he had any last words for loved ones.

"I must not forget Mother," he said, reaching back with his right arm to a leather-bound packet one of the stretcher bearers had placed under his head. With my attendants supporting him and myself steadying his hand, he penned several lines to his mother, dabbing a corner of the missive into his wound before handing it to me. If I thought I had already witnessed a miracle of heart and mind transcending the mortal dictates of this world, I was even more astounded by what happened next.

By now, several groups of stretcher bearers and walking wounded had silently gathered around us. Jeremiah, taking the cup of black drop from my hand, addressed us thusly: "Boys, it seems you can't toast me, but I will toast you. To you, our Confederacy and to Victory!" A short sip, the cup returned and the youth expired, being laid gently back on the stretcher. Our company, now numbering about fifty, stood with eyes transfixed upon this flower of Southern manhood. The bombardment seemed to cease and fade off into another dimension although we found later it had not and indeed was but half over. It will be a poorer American society that survives this war,

Sally, if such noble spirits are expended in fighting it. For
my part . . . [7]

Three

It is important you keep between the enemy and the Capital.

> —General Halleck to General Meade

Back at First Corps Headquarters where the hands of pocket watches read 7:30 A.M., General Longstreet began explaining his alternatives to Pickett's Charge by placing his engineer's map of the battlefield before General Lee—

The devolution of our army around the enemy's left will proceed from north to south along our line on Seminary Ridge. Our objective in so doing will be to draw him off his strengthened position in our front—which is of minor strategic importance to our cause—by first threatening his capital and subsequently his army via prepared positions interposed between the two in central Maryland (Map below).

The key to the successful execution of this movement is twofold: 1. *Concentration of Artillery Fire* on Culp's Hill and Little Round Top to allow disengagement of our most forward infantry divisions. 2. *Rapidity of Movement* to the southeast after the last elements of our army clears the left flank of the enemy on the Round Tops.

Acceptance and implementation of the above remains the sole responsibility of the Commanding General and communications regarding the same would emanate only from General Headquarters through the respective Corps Commanders.

After a lingering glance at the map, Lee would straighten and look pensively at his First Corps Commander before speaking: "You know, General Longstreet, I note a distinct contrast between your optimism for this plan and the pessimism you share with General Hill regarding a frontal assault against the enemy center. Have you given any thought, however, as to how this army would feed itself on a march toward Washington?"

"Sir," Longstreet would recall answering in support of his alternative, "We still have the three thousand head of cattle and numerous wagons of provisions secured by General Ewell since crossing the Potomac. Just last night, General Hood reported troops in his forward lines possessing haversacks full of 'good Pennsylvania grub.'[1] More importantly, Harrison has informed me that Meade moved large stores of supplies to the Pipe Creek area in Maryland which would be ours for the taking."

Lee, who distrusted spies in general and Harrison in particular, would smile wanly as he reached for Traveler's reins; "Very well, General. I will issue the appropriate orders to Generals Ewell, Hill and Stuart. Make yourself available at Army Headquarters by nine o'clock for final consultation on their implementation."

Responsibility for initiating Longstreet's alternative to Pickett's Charge would fall to the Second Corps Commander, Richard Stoddert Ewell, who commanded the Confederate left (northernmost position), which stretched in a two-mile area below the town of Gettysburg. Acceding to Corps Command after the death of

Stonewall Jackson and the reorganization of the Army of
Northern Virginia, which had followed, Ewell had recently been criticized by Lee because he "could not or
would not" push his July 1st advantage by driving "those
people" of the hills to his front. Now, in "Listening to Old
Pete" at Lee's Headquarters, and in glancing once more
at Lee's disengagement order, he probably strove mightily not to view each as further criticism of his failure to
carry Cemetery and Culp's Hill two days before. Nonetheless, if the missing leg of "Old Baldy" represented anything, it was his refusal to wallow long in the luxury of
self-pity. On this July 3rd, he would extricate his "people"
and lead them toward Washington, D.C., just as they had
led the Army of Northern Virginia into Pennsylvania several days ago.

Summoning first his artillery commander, Lieutenant Colonel Thomas H. Carter, Ewell handed him the
"half-wheel" sketch he had drawn back at headquarters.

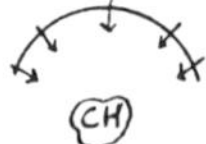

"It seems Colonel that our guns have been too dispersed. Bring the twelve batteries of our command to
Brenner's Hill and arrange them thusly with their line of
fire concentrated on Culp's Hill.[2] At noon, you will commence firing in a way that obscures all further view of the
enemy trenches. Your guns will be both the signal to our
army that a devolution to the right is under way and a
cover under which the divisions of Johnson and Early will
withdraw to the Hanover Road. I will assign Colonel Ave-
ry's regiment to support your guns." As Carter saluted
and galloped off, Ewell would turn to the caped officer riding beside him. "General Stuart, I thank you for accompa-

nying me and providing a recitation of your role in support of the Second Corps."

J. E. B. Stuart, of Cavalier plume and twinkling eye, had as much reason as Ewell to regain the confidence of his commanding general. His official battle song, composed by a ragtail group of musicians ensconced in his entourage, contained a third line that could well describe the meeting he had with Lee on July 2nd:

If you want to smell hell—
If you want to have fun—
If you want to catch the Devil—
Jine the cavalry!

Stuart raised himself in the stirrups and pointed to the Hanover Road junction that came up from Rock Creek and along which Johnson's heavily-engaged division would soon withdraw westward through Gettysburg—

"My cavalry will screen General Johnson's withdrawal along that road from any Federal pursuit. At noon, I will present my division along the left of General Gordon's brigade and order my horse artillery to engage Steven's batteries between Culp's and Cemetery Hill. General Gordon will then make an aggressive feint forward on the right of these guns as if to engage the extreme left of the Federal line. The rest of my division meanwhile, aided by its light artillery—dismounting if necessary—will move against Wadsworth's infantry units placed in that swale between the two hills. These actions should not only screen Johnson's withdrawal from harassment, but will serve to disguise his withdrawal as an attempt to support our units attacking Cemetery Hill on his right."

With an exchange of salutes, this Ewell-Stuart conference would end somewhere between 10:45 and 11:00 A.M. on July 3rd. This conference, however, reflects not just the careful attention to detail that characterized Longstreet's battle plans, but also the necessary ignorance of Meade's intentions for the Army of the Potomac recorded before and after July 3, 1863. As already indicated, the Council of War that Meade convened for the night of July 2nd, had called for the Union Army to remain in a fixed, defensive position awaiting a Southern attack throughout July 3rd. In addition, even after the obvious failure of Pickett's Charge that afternoon, the historical record shows that as late as July 4th, Meade's generals were under orders to avoid resistance to any retrograde movements of the Confederate Army.[3]

These orders would allow the Army of Northern Virginia to not only disengage from the battlefield without being counterattacked, but to march for half-a-week with a wagon train of wounded seventeen miles long to encounter an unfordable river without experiencing any significant combat or reconnaissance mission by its adversary—a fact that left President Lincoln "a good deal dissatisfied." For our purpose of analyzing the immediate effects Old Pete's Alternative would have on Meade's army, therefore, the observation by Edwin Fishel in *The Secret War for the Union* is meaningful, i.e.,

Meade's caution was partly due to uncertainty as to whether Lee was intending retreat to Virginia or *maneuvering for a favorable position to receive an attack he would expect Meade to make.*[4]

Meanwhile, over on Seminary Ridge, Ambrose Powell Hill, whose battlefield persona stood in direct contrast to that of Longstreet, would undoubtedly be fuming over the latter's alternative for July 3rd. Whereas Longstreet was a meticulous planner for battle, Hill was impetuous for engaging the enemy; now as Longstreet was "maneuvering for a favorable position to receive an attack," it was Hill's natural aggressiveness in donning his Red Shirt that had started this fight at Gettysburg in the first place. Probably no other corps commander in the field, therefore, was more psychologically committed to directing a successful (Pickett's) charge to his front than was A.P. Hill, for it would be both a personal and historical vindication that his Third Corps could finish what it had started two days before. In this respect, both the historical record (Pickett's Charge) and the historical alternative (Longstreet's disengagement) coincide in disappointing Hill. His subsequent failure to inform key brigades to support Pickett "en echelon" was probably reflective of his chagrin in being denied overall responsibility for the attack.[5] Now, the shortest of all three orders issued by Lee for the alternative was simply a marching order without any tactical responsibilities whatsoever. Sullenly, Hill would turn over such an order to his adjutant for transmission to division commanders:

> Continue all skirmishing duties until 2:30 P.M. When the last Second Corps division (Rodes) passes behind our right, fall in the marching order of Anderson, Heth and Pender.

At First Corps Headquarters, Lieutenant General James Longstreet would be eagerly preparing to sanctify the faith Lee had finally placed in his alternative to a frontal assault. First Corps would be the important hinge upon which the southeasterly swing of the Army of Northern Virginia would first turn toward Washington,

and then slam shut between that city and its defenders
bloodlessly forced from their stronghold on Cemetery
Ridge. Indeed, one more "Fredericksburg" in central
Maryland and the peace mission of the Confederacy's
Vice-President might bear immediate fruit. As Longstreet waited for the arrival of his artillery chief, Colonel
E. Porter Alexander, the noon hour struck suddenly with
the opening roar of Ewell's guns arrayed on Brenner's
Hill and the portal slowly began to move in Old Pete's direction. Taking a blank page handed him by an orderly,
Longstreet sketched two halves of a wagon wheel at the
top of each corner and handed it to Alexander as the latter dismounted seconds later. Exchanging salutes, the final orders for initiating the alternative to Pickett's
Charge were issued:

"Colonel, these sketches are replicas of the one provided General Ewell this morning for his opening artillery practice on Culp's Hill. The directions concerning
your fire mission are so critical for the successful devolution of this army that you will write them as I direct, stopping me the moment you have a question;

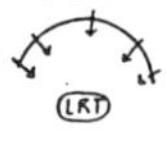

1. By 2 P.M. our artillery must be arranged in two semi-
   circles so as to concentrate their fire on the
   summits of Little and Big Round Tops as
   designated above.[5]
2. Since it is under this fire and through these two positions that the divisions of McLaws and Hood will
   withdraw, these two positions will be 100 yards northwest of Devil's Den and approximately 200 yards
   southeast of the Peach Orchard respectively.
3. General Pickett's Division will be deployed in support
   of your guns and will provide your rear guard and that

of our army during its march south on the Emmitsburg Road—time subject to development of #2.

4. I will order General Barksdale in one hour to push McCandless's Brigade back toward Little Round Top so as not to harass this withdrawal.

"Any questions?"

"None, sir," Alexander would reply. "My batteries can be in position by 1:45 P.M."

By 1:45 P.M., the rear elements of Ewell's Second Corps (i.e., Rodes's division) would be filing south off the Hagerstown Road into the lane behind Seminary Ridge just taken by the divisions of Johnson and Early. To Federal observers from Cemetery Hill to the base of Little Round Top three miles distant, only two reasons could be offered for the move now taking place: a) a reinforced attack against the Union enter on Cemetery Ridge or b) a reinforced attack against the Union left on Little Round Top. For a brief fifteen minutes, the vigorous skirmishing kept up by Hill's Third Corps conjoined with the rising dust of Ewell's three divisions heading toward this center of the rebel line seemed to support the first option.

Ironically, it would fall to the oldest unit in the United States Army to discern the fallacy of the above two explanations. Battery D, Fifth United States Artillery, a lineal descendant of Alexander Hamilton's battery at Trenton, had been the first to gain the heights of Little Round Top in response to Gouverneur Warren's last-minute order that had saved the Union left on July 2nd. According to General Hunt, Meade's Artillery Commander,

The passage of the guns through the roadless woods and amongst the rocks was marvelous. Under ordinary circumstances it would have been considered an impossible feat, but the eagerness of the men to get into action . . . and the skilled driving brought them without delay to the very summit where they went immediately into battle. They were barely in time for the enemy were also climbing the hill.[6]

Now, Lieutenant Rittenhouse and the other survivors of Battery D were the first bluecoats to see Alexander's batteries forming in two large concentric circles between the Peach Orchard and Devil's Den on the fields below; they would be the first bluecoats to see the deployment of Pickett's fresh division east of the Emmittsburg Road in support of those guns. If these two deployments indicated a renewed attack against the Round Tops, however, neither Rittenhouse nor the rest of Sykes's Fifth Corps would have had much time to relay that suspicion to units on their right because at two P.M., these nineteen batteries erupted in an ear-deafening salvo against their position. The seventy-two guns of Huger's, Muller's, and Dearing's batteries firing en enfilade across the crest of Little Round Top seemed to—in the sarcastic phrase used by one of Hill's gunners earlier that morning—"decapitate" the spot where Battery D had stood so proudly the day before. Meanwhile, the men of Hood's and McLaws's Divisions, aware for twenty-four hours that Federal guns could not be depressed sharply enough to contest their withdrawal, from the hillside, began streaming through Pickett's cheering ranks to formations in the rear. Lost to the immediate view of Sykes's men was the emergence of Ewell's Corps from the lane behind Seminary Ridge, heading south on the Emmittsburg Road toward a far different objective.

By three o'clock on July 3rd, the time history records

Pickett's division deploying for their fateful assault on Cemetery Ridge, Longstreet's alternative had completed the withdrawal of its brother divisions from the Round Tops through prearranged gaps in the still-fresh unit. As the weary Texans and Alabamians passed through to the rear, Pickett's staff officers congratulated them for "treeing the Yankees so we can march on to Washington." Alexander's guns would keep up their "practice" for one more hour until these men had been fed, rested and their wounded placed in ambulances bound for Virginia. It would also be about four P.M. when the advance elements of Hill's Third Corps began filing out on to the Emmittsburg Road in the direction already taken by Ewell.

To the Union observers, the slackening of Alexander's cannonade, coinciding with the sudden appearance of Hill's corps moving along Longstreet's rear did little to dispel the possibility of a reenforced attack on their left. It would only be near the advanced hour of six P.M. when the ranks of First Corps, freshly dressed, discounted a renewed attack against the Union left by executing a right face to follow the rest of the Southern army toward Emmittsburg, Maryland. At that time, the last remaining scenario more feared by Meade and Halleck than a frontal assault "wig-wagged" its way back to Army Headquarters via the red and white flags of the Federal Signal Corps.

As pointed out above, the successful disengagement by the Army of Northern Virginia from the Gettysburg battlefield probably owes as much to the intentions of Meade as to the completeness of Longstreet's planning. Here again there is a strong coincidence between the historical record of the rebel army's departure and our analysis of the Longstreet alternative to that record. As Edwin Fishel notes in his *The Secret War for the Union,*

Although the Confederates could not hide their march, it was NOT well-covered by Meade's scouts or cavalry; the citizens' scouting and spying that had served so well before the battle were sorely missed. Cavalry reconnaissance was Meade's most promising source, but the supply of horses was being depleted so seriously as to threaten the movement of the whole army.[7]

In short, for both the historical record and the historical alternative to that record, the overriding question for Meade remained the same: was Lee retreating to Virginia or "maneuvering for a favorable position to receive an attack he would expect Meade to make?"

Departing the Visitors' Center at the Gettysburg National Military Park today, the "average" visitor (native and foreign-born) has probably been treated at least once to the Ted Turner interpretation of the Lee-Longstreet debate regarding the tactics to be employed on July 3, 1863. To follow "Old Pete's" alternative down the Emmittsburg Road with us, however, it becomes necessary for such a visitor to jettison his/her memory of a wild-eyed Martin Sheen (as Lee) proclaiming to our protagonist, "I have never left the enemy in possession of the field." In point of fact, Lee had done just that ten months earlier and fifty miles to the southwest at Antietam, Maryland, after the war's bloodiest single day when a reasoned reappraisal of the tactical situation required it.

Now, at the site of the present-day traffic circle in Emmittsburg; Maryland (ten miles southwest of the Round Tops), the veterans of Antietam would be reminded by their officers that unlike the road taken after that battle, the road ahead—today's Route 140—led toward Baltimore and Washington. Most certainly, it would be along this Emmitsburg-Taneytown Road that Lee would feel the time and place was ripe for consultation with his three corps commanders.

While Meade's Army of the Potomac celebrated the eighty-seventh birthday of the United States, the fall of Vicksburg and the immediate repulse of Lee's veterans, the bedraggled corps commanders of those veterans began arriving at temporary headquarters in Taneytown as their rain-soaked columns marched by outside. Probably by now Longstreet's face would mirror the anxiety of a man whose urgings had been responsible for the redeployment of those columns into a countryside with which he was not personally familiar. He might even have contemplated initiating an immediate inquiry as to whether Stuart's cavalry had been sent ahead to scout for a favorable defensive position from which these columns could once again repulse the Army of the Potomac. If so, he was probably dissuaded by Lee's opening comments, which indicated—according to the historical record—that Stuart had already accomplished this mission back on June 30th when his division moved north through Union Mills, Maryland, the very center of Meade's chosen defensive line at Pipe Creek.[8] As protocol would dictate, Lee opened the conference with a brief summation, which related the alternative chosen to the historical record of the Pennsylvania campaign.

Gentlemen, as you know, the engagement of our Army with the enemy on July 1st and 2nd, was undertaken without the necessary intelligence gained by General Stuart's Cavalry. An army thus deprived of its "eyes and ears" can not expect, even under ordinary circumstances, to prevail against a superior force strongly entrenched on its home soil. It has been decided by me, therefore, to reposition our army according to the extensive intelligence gained for it by General Stuart's reconnaissance prior to the onset of hostilities at Gettysburg. My decision had been arrived at due in no small part to General Longstreet's patient admonitions as to the wisdom of such a re-deployment. I will now ask Colonel Taylor to read a dispatch captured by General Stuart from one of General Meade's couriers prior to the engagement at Hanover.

Headquarters, Army of the Potomac
Taneytown, July 1, 1863

To Corps Commanders,

. . . the Commanding General is satisfied that the object of the movement of the army in this direction has been accomplished via, the relief of Harrisburg and the prevention of the enemy's intended invasion of Philadelphia and beyond the Susquehanna. It is no longer his intention to assume the offensive until the enemy's movement or *position* should render such an operation certain of success . . . it is his intention . . . to withdraw the army from its' present position (i.e., Gettysburg) and form a line of battle with the left resting in the neighborhood of Middleburg and the right at Manchester (Maryland), the *general direction of Pipe Creek* (see MAP below). For this purpose, General Reynolds in command of the left will *withdraw the force (II Corps) currently at Gettysburg* by the road to Taneytown and Westminster and, after crossing Pipe Creek, deploy toward Middleburg.

General Slocum (XII Corps) will assume command of the two corps at Hanover and Two Taverns and withdraw via Union Mills deploying one to the right and one to the

left with General Reynolds and his right to General Sedgwick at Manchester who will connect to form our right.

S. Williams
Assistant Adjutant General
Army of the Potomac
(Official Records I part 3).[9]

The impetuous A. P. Hill would likely be the first to speak. "It would seem, Sir, that we have stolen much more than a day's march on General Meade. We are also about to take possession of his preferred defensive position as well." Since the southern columns were now only about three miles from Big Pipe Creek, Lee probably would have demurred to Hill on this point. "To this end," continued Lee, "my staff has prepared copies of the MAP captured from General Meade's courier for each of you. Our deployment on the heights south of Pipe Creek[10] will be made in reference to it."

General Ewell, since II Corps will reach Pipe Creek first, it is imperative that you block the road from Union Mills as early as practicable. Accordingly, you will turn to the left after crossing and assume the high ground from that road east to Manchester, commanding the right of our army (the role given in the above dispatch to Sedgwick). Most of your artillery should be placed to cover the crossing at Union Mills since I expect Meade to be arriving from that quarter. Meanwhile, I have already directed General Stuart to cover the deployment of our army from the north bank of Pipe Creek. When his lead brigade reaches Manchester, it will be detached southward to sever the rail line of the Western Maryland railroad as it crosses Parr's Ridge to our rear.

General Hill, being second in line of march, your corps will be responsible for our center. Accordingly, you

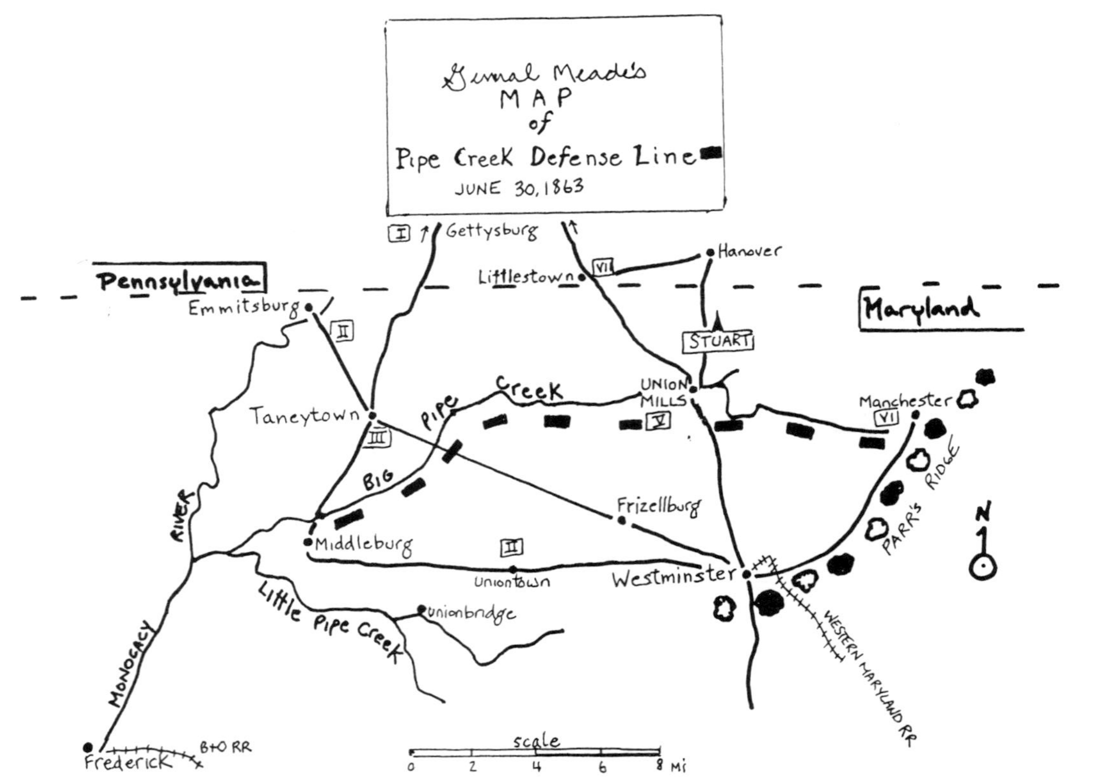
General Meade's
MAP
of
Pipe Creek Defense Line
JUNE 30, 1863
Pennsylvania
Maryland
I Gettysburg
Hanover
Littlestown
VI
STUART
Emmitsburg
II
Creek
Pipe
UNION MILLS
Manchester
VII
Taneytown
III
V
BIG
Frizellburg
Middleburg
II
Uniontown
Westminster
Unionbridge
PARR'S RIDGE
N
RIVER
Little Pipe Creek
WESTERN MARYLAND RR
MONOCACY
B+O RR
Frederick
scale
0   2   4   6   8 Mi

too will turn left after crossing Pipe Creek and connect your right flank with the left of General Ewell on the road coming up to your position from Union Mills. Your artillery should be so arranged with General Ewell's as to provide an enfilade of the road leading up from Union Mills. Your left will extend to the northernmost bend of Pipe Creek, six miles west of this road and connect with the right flank of First Corps.

General Longstreet, your corps will reach Pipe Creek last and be deployed west toward Middleburg forming the left of our army, your right connecting with General Hill's left. If General Meade decides to engage our army from the route it is now taking, your corps will have the primary responsibility of frustrating this objective.

Gentlemen, it is now nine A.M., July 4th. By this time tomorrow, my staff and I shall begin inspecting your selection of earthworks for the upcoming contest. Our strategic objective here is twofold: 1. To punish all attacks launched by the enemy and 2. In so doing, to pose such a threat to his capital in our rear, that maximum credibility will be afforded the peace initiative of our government and its ultimate cause of Southern Independence. If there are no questions, you are dismissed.

By the early morning of July 7th, George Gordon Meade had probably accepted the unwelcome prognosis of what A. P. Hill had observed three days before—the Army of Northern Virginia was now in possession of his chosen defensive line below Big Pipe Creek, Maryland. A subsequent and stronger cavalry patrol sent down the Baltimore Road toward Union Mills on July 6th had not only clashed with Stuart's cavalry north of the crossing, but observed through field glasses gray-clad infantry heavily entrenched along heights south of the creek that his own artillery commander had earlier pronounced a formidable "offensive-defensive line."[11]

Was this to be another Fredericksburg? Meade would probably try to convince himself that it could not be for both strategic and tactical reasons. The Southern army, in "Listening to Old Pete," had placed itself between the nation's capital and the Army of the Potomac. An attack had to be made, but there could be no "going back" as Burnside had done seven months earlier. From this twin realization was determined the nature of the question Meade placed before a Council of War held at his Gettysburg headquarters on the afternoon of July 7th: "How can an attack be launched against Lee's strongly-entrenched veterans, while avoiding both the devastating results of such a tactic in the past as well as the more important effects such a result would presently have on the fate of the nation's capital?"

It would become obvious to most of Meade's Corps Commanders—some sooner than others—that from the very nature of his question, the Army of the Potomac would have to be divided: One large contingent to attack the Confederate Army entrenched along Pipe Creek and the other to get below the Southern army to form a defense of Washington, D.C. By five P.M., July 7th, Meade's general orders for an offensive against his own previously-chosen defensive line at Pipe Creek was in the hands of his corps commanders: viz

Headquarters, Army of the Potomac
Gettysburg, Pennsylvania
July 7, 1863

————commanding ——Corps,
Since the repulse of the enemy at this place four days ago, their army has re-deployed to defensive positions below Pipe creek approximately 15 miles distant. Since the

mission of this army is twofold: a) Repulse enemy forces from states loyal to the Union and b) Protection of the nation's capital at Washington, the following corps disposition is hereby ordered preparatory to a general engagement.

1. The XI (Howard) and XII (Slocum) Corps will depart Gettysburg east via the Gettysburg & Hanover Railroad as soon as sufficient transport is available (preferably no later than July 12th) to the junction with the Western Maryland Railroad.

    a) Preceding south on the Western Maryland Railroad, General Howard will establish telegraph communication with General Halleck upon reaching the spur to Westminster (i.e. the enemy's rear).

    b) Conveying this General's preference that the XI and XII Corps be deployed for engagement in the enemy's rear, General Howard will nonetheless place these corps under General Halleck's command for the defense of Washington or Baltimore if the latter so directs.

2. The III (Hancock) and V (Sykes) Corps will proceed at dawn, July 8th to Taneytown via the Taneytown Road. At Taneytown, these corps will depart for Pipe Creek (s/east) along the route taken by the enemy. Since these units will constitute the right flank of any attack against the Pipe Creek Line, both the 1st (Buford) and 2nd (Gregg) divisions of cavalry will be placed at General Hancock's disposal for reconnaissance and communication with Army Headquarters traveling along the Baltimore Road.

3. The Ist (Doubleday) IInd (Hays) and VIth (Sedgwick) Corps, along with headquarters, will proceed at dawn (July 8th) toward Union Mills via

Battle of Pipe Creek/Union Mills, Md.

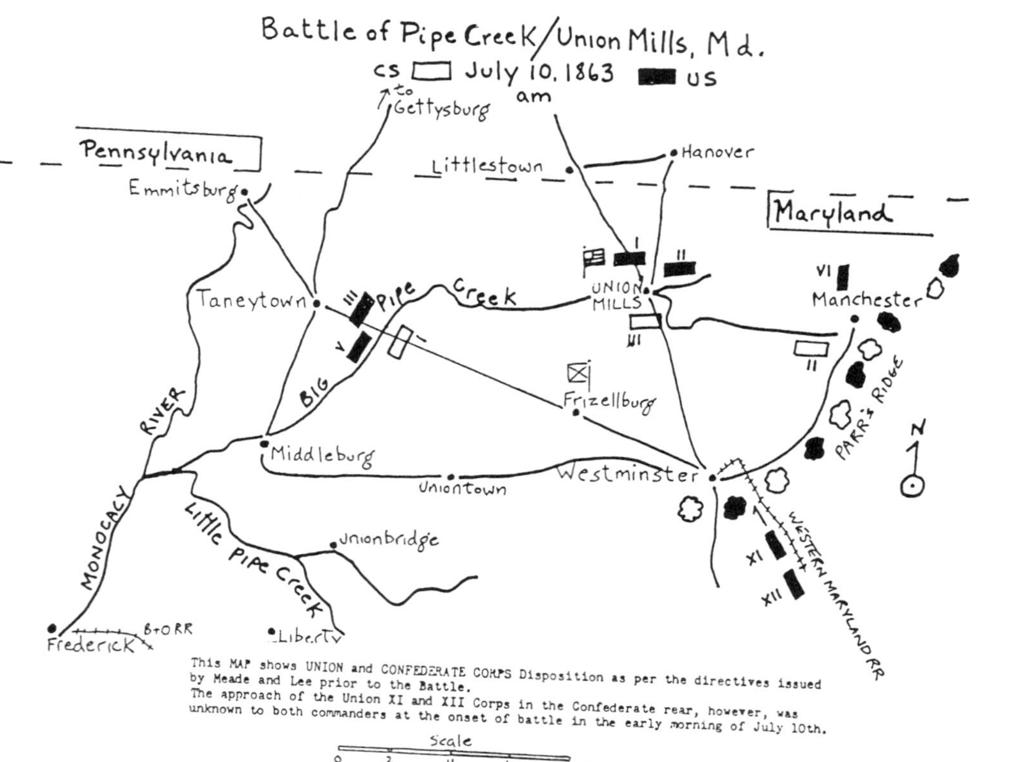

This MAP shows UNION and CONFEDERATE CORPS Disposition as per the directives issued by Meade and Lee prior to the Battle.
The approach of the Union XI and XII Corps in the Confederate rear, however, was unknown to both commanders at the onset of battle in the early morning of July 10th.

the Baltimore Road, the 3rd (Kilpatrick) division
of cavalry performing reconnaissance duties.
   a) Union Mills, once secured, will constitute
      Army Headquarters at the approximate
      center of the Pipe Creek Line.
   b) VI Corps (Sedgwick) will be deployed east
      toward Manchester forming the left of
      this army during a general engagement.
4. Corps Commanders (excepting XI & XII) are expected to confirm the above dispositions with headquarters no later than nine A.M., July 9th.

General Meade,
Commanding, Army of the Potomac

(See MAP p. 46 for above Corps dispositions.)

My memory of the Battle of Union Mills—or Pipe Creek as the Yankees called it—starts with this view our

University Grays had trudging along the Taneytown-Westminster Road in the pouring rain shortly after noon on July 4, 1863. Of course, the sign was placed here long after the battle as were many objects in the stream that would have kept us from filling our empty canteens on that steamy Independence afternoon. Yes, sir, it was water from above and water from below that day, but if "Old Pete" was looking for another Fredericksburg, we all could see that Big Pipe Creek was no Ranahannock River. Of course, this rather somber observation brightened considerably as we began to ascend the heights south of the stream.

The road was narrow, bordered by dense woods and the heights we finally gained left even the fittest men in our company short of breath. As more of our division gained the heights, from the privates to the generals, all could see that any army attacking up these hills against entrenched positions would be severely punished in so doing. I've provided you a picture of my observations looking back north along the route we had taken from Gettysburg.

If Meade had preferred swapping this view for the one he had of our boys from Cemetery Ridge, we Rebs (and especially yours truly) got the better of that swap! Since this particular view and road, however, were to be defended by Longstreet's corps coming up behind us, we rested only a few minutes before turning left (east) to take our position eight miles distant guarding the Union Mills–Westminster Road in the center of our line. This part of Maryland abounds in fruit trees and other farm commodities, so in their double role as harvesters of nature's bounty, our Grays only reached the site for their trenches about five P.M. We were butted up against the left of Ewell's Second Corps (Rodes's division), which had

arrived earlier in the day and had already begun their digging in a way that would provide an enveloping, plunging fire in cooperation with our division (still under the command of General Pettigrew) of the road coming up from Union Mills. (See MAP p. 46.)

The five days that intervened between our arrival on the heights overlooking Pipe Creek and the appearance of bluecoats north of the stream, were a strange mixture of pain and pleasure. The most ferocious digging and tree-hauling tasks for the improvement of our works during the morning and early afternoon were followed by luxurious dips in Pipe creek later in the day and early evening. Lifeguarding duties were left to Stuart's cavalry, whose brigades were much in evidence between us and the Yankees, but who nonetheless fired good-natured barbs at us about the infantry getting caught with their trousers down by the slow-moving Meade. I firmly believe that the juxtaposition of this daily routine, along with successful foraging ventures after dark, left our army more hardy and refreshed than at any time during its northern incursion. By July 9, 1863, with the bluecoats arriving in greater numbers, the swimming stopped and serious skirmishing began.

As it turned out, the Battle of Union Mills (CS) or Pipe Creek (US) fought on July 10 and 11, 1863, had four distinct stages, which were characteristic of the entire War Between the States. Let me identify these stages for the reader of this narrative and then provide this participant's view of each stage:

1. (July 10 A.M.) Repulse of simultaneous Union attacks against well-entrenched Confederate positions.
2. (July 10 P.M.) Railroads used by Union to place additional troops to the south (rear) of Confederate positions.
3. (July 11 A.M.) The tactical expertise of Lee in thwarting the threat posed by #2.
4. (July 11 P.M.) Exploitation of weakened Confederate right flank via #3 by superior Union numbers.

I was awakened before dawn on July 10th by sporadic rifle fire over to our left, which quickly increased in volume and intensity. We had heard two days ago that, for old time's sake, General Longstreet had placed Barksdale's Mississippians down by the Taneytown crossing of Pipe Creek to contest any attempt by the bluecoats to launch an attack at the bridge/ford pictured above. Well, if Old Pete was determined to reenact Fredericksburg here along Pipe Creek, our Third Corps had some props to contribute to the scenery as well. Our artillery, which had "clicked in" on the Union Mills crossing below, was the Fredericksburg Battery commanded by Captain E. A. Marye, a member of that family from whose heights the Confederates repelled Burnside's army back in December 1862.[12] It seemed this battery went into action the minute I dove head first and half-awake into our trench, which was only about ten yards from the old apple tree under which I had spent the night. Despite my cobwebs and the heavy smoke raised by Captain Marye's battery—now joined by the rest of Peagram's battalion and some of Ewell's guns on the other side of the road—it was clear Meade was pushing simultaneous attacks against us from both major crossings.

By mid-morning, one could discern a definite contrast in how our left and center were responding to Meade's twofold attack. In the center, where our Grays were stationed, the artillery maintained mastery of the road leading up to our trenches from Meade's headquarters one mile distant at Union Mills. The Confederate cannonade here was, as I noted above, both enveloping and plunging.

Consequently, shortly after crossing the creek below, under intense fire, lead elements of the Yankee First and Second Corps (Doubleday's and Hay's) realized that the narrow road leading up to our trenches was a rebel bowling alley with them as the perfectly-aligned pins. When this realization caused them to file off the road to form a line of battle in the woods, however, their formations were broken both by the heavily-wooded terrain and the rain of heavy timbers created by the enfilade of our batteries on either side of the road. There was little for our Grays to do that morning other than duck those occasional Federal shells that skipped over our trenches on the carom. It appeared that our elevation was so high and our earthworks so extensive that we had little to fear from Yankee artillerists on the north side of Pipe Creek. We had no way of knowing then that our spectator role in this position would end at noon, but from where we stood in the morning, it appeared that Meade was determined to "out-Burnside, Burnside" in our center.

Over on our left, meanwhile, intense rifle fire continued to characterize our First Corp's defense, with only occasional bursts from Alexander's artillery. We learned later that two factors were responsible for this contrast: a) Alexander's ammunition had been sorely depleted during the disengagement from Little Round Top on July 3rd, and b) Old Pete had ordered the rest of McLaws's Division to pattern their defense of the Taneytown approach after the one initially used by Barksdale's Brigade—the "plunging V."

The "plunging V" was a tactic generally well-suited for an infantry defense of roads and particularly well-suited for the terrain in front of our trenches above Pipe Creek. The apex of the V, consisting of two Whitworth rifled cannon supported by sharpshooters, was on the road clearly visible to the approaching enemy column, but farthest from them. The "arms" of the V (consisting of Kershaw's brigade on the left and Semmes on the right) ran down diagonally through the woods with troops protected by fallen trees specially selected by engineers. When elements of Hancock's Third Corps had crossed Pipe Creek at dawn, they sought cover from the highly accurate fire coming from the road's summit by taking to the woods on their flank—much as their comrades had done in our center.

Almost immediately, however, they had come under

a withering fire from the diagonal lines of protected infantry in the woods. All morning long, General Longstreet orchestrated this plunging V "dance" against first Hancock and then Syke's corps. While two brigades manned the "hot arms" of the V, one rested in the trenches. Both Hood on the right and Pickett on the left of the road had been ordered to support either arm of McLaws if it was in danger of being overrun by the Yankees. Unlike the Yankee imperative to form lines of battle in the woods to attack frontally or to their flank, however, this support simply called for a mad rush down the hill to man prepared barricades. In this manner, both the able Hancock and the formerly proud defender of Little Round Top were kept at bloody bay throughout the morning of July 10, 1863.

Now I don't mean to convey the impression that all the news on July 10th was rosey. About noon, General Lee appeared behind our trenches for a conference with General Hill and we learned through the grapevine that both had expressed major concerns about the morning's events—the most important being that Meade had only committed four of his seven available corps to the attack thus far. Although there was no major road leading up to General Ewell's position on our right, things had been strangely quiet all along his front (with the exception of Rodes's artillery units, which had been helping us control the road from Union Mills). In this regard, Lee ordered a more equalized defense between our center and left through a slackening of our heavy reliance on artillery and the transfer of some ordinance over to Longstreet's corps. As a result of this adjustment, our role as infantry spectators ended and we were ordered forward into the woods to re-create Old Pete's chosen defense with our axes. I must have shed twenty pounds on that hot July afternoon since it was only in swinging those axes that we could drown out the horrible groans and screams of Yankee wounded still pinned down and draped across the blasted timber below us. Occasionally, we dragged the most pitiful of these out onto the road where they tried to crawl down to the relative safety of their picket line along the now-bloody Pipe Creek. By five P.M., our hellish duty as sappers ended and we returned to our trenches for a welcome supper of roasted corn and fruit. It was now obvious that Meade, whose casualties, must have been extremely heavy, would make no more attempt to storm our heights that day.

Regretfully, as the dawn of July 11th broke over Parr's Ridge, we Confederates soon learned the whereabouts of Howard's and Slocum's Corps (XI and XII). Stuart's cavalry patrols had sighted large numbers of bluecoats disembarking from trains along the Western Maryland spur to Westminster at the point where his men had earlier terminated their track-wrecking duties. This point was about seven miles behind our lines and east of the Gap, which led through Parr's Ridge. We learned further after the war that both Lincoln and Halleck had agreed with Meade that these two corps could serve the double purpose of operating against our rear and still be in a position to fall back in defense of Washington if things didn't work out as planned. Now, however, if these two corps were allowed to come up one or both of the roads leading to our rear, the Army of Northern Virginia would be trapped between a rock and a hard place.

As you probably know by now, dear Reader, the history of this conflict abounds with instances similar to the above and, but for the tactical genius of General Lee, the superior quantity of Northern manpower, railroad mileage and ordinance might have shortened the conflict by a considerable number of years. Neither Lee, the hard facts of history, or Longstreet's alternative to that history, however, was ready to write that chapter for our army on July 11, 1863. If Old Pete had gotten his Fredericksburg on the tenth, Lee was about to take a page out of Chancellorsville to underwrite its success.

Tactical operations south of our line between Westminster and Parr Ridge Gap for the rest of July 11, 1863 are described in the following chronology:

The first order of business was to plug the Gap leading through Parr's Ridge to Westminster as soon as possible. Lee ordered the whole of Stuart's Cavalry Division to execute this first order. It must have been shortly before seven A.M. when we began hearing the echoes of Stuart's horse artillery going into action at what we thought was the extreme western mouth of the Gap. Weeks later, we learned that Stuart had actually—and daringly—placed his guns one half mile into the gap toward the approaching Union columns. Meanwhile, the rest of the division, by foot and horse, had arranged themselves forward of the guns along the heavily-wooded northern and southern slopes of Parr Ridge Gap.

As the columns of Howard and Slocum attempted to penetrate the gap, they were met by a serious artillery fire to their front and a plunging, highly-accurate carbine ambuscade on the right and left of their line of march. The deeper the Yankee XI and XII Corps sought to penetrate this gap (through which the ruined track-bed of the Western Maryland ran), the hotter our fun-loving cavalier made it for them.

Meanwhile, preparatory to the Yankees inevitable forcing the gap via their superior numbers and firepower, Lee ordered Old Pete to speed his freshest division down the Taneytown-Westminster Road to establish a defensive line along the now-defunct railroad embankment that turns abruptly southwest after clearing Parr Ridge Gap to link up with Westminster a mile and a half away. By nine A.M., so we learned, Pickett's division, which had been spared offensive operations at Gettysburg, was in place behind the railroad embankment utilizing the once-useless railroad ties to develop a strongly-fortified base of fire. Lee had also instructed Pickett once he arrived, to employ every device for inflating his true numbers to the approaching bluecoats much as the former had done in checking Hooker at Chancellorsville. The most bizarre of these involved the unheard of borrowing of decommissioned banners from other First Corps units which were carried far to the left and right behind the embankment by lightly-wounded members of Stuart's division as they fell back to this temporary shelter from their action in the gap.

The third part of Lee's plan to counter the threat to our rear on July 11, was the most daring. Once the Yankees had engaged Pickett's "masquerade corps" behind its fortified railroad embankment running southwest toward Westminster, two divisions pulled down from Ewell's quiet front to the north would suddenly attack the entire right flank of the enemy, "crossing the T" with their battle line so to speak. The timing for the arrival of Johnson's and Early's division at this juncture was so critical, that Lee posted Stuart's staff at the exact point on the Manchester-Westminster Road that would keep them undetected by the Yankees until the latter were fully committed against Pickett's fortified line. By the volume of fire that reached our Grays on the heights overlooking Pipe Creek, it sounded like this commitment began shortly before noon.

Things were relatively quiet on our front opposite Union Mills at this time except for the occasional sniper fire down near the crossing. Either Meade did not care to launch a simultaneous attack on our front by midday or else he was waiting for more definitive reports of progress by Howard and Slocum before doing so. At any rate, a difference of opinion exists to this day as to what we heard next coming from the southeast. Some of my old comrades from the brigade swear they first heard the rebel yell rolling up from Johnson's and Early's divisions as they lit into Howard's right flank down by the gap. Others swear just as earnestly that they heard the sounds of DIXIE coming from the small band of musicians that seemed to accompany Stuart wherever he went.

To tell you the truth, I heard a brief intermingling of both sounds just before they were drowned out by the loudest coordinated crash of musketry that met my ears since Sharpsburg. In an irony lost on no one in our ranks, we learned that General Johnson had placed the Stonewall Brigade (the second, fourth, fifth, twenty-seventh, and thirty-third Virginia Regiments) directly in the center of his battle line as it hit Howard's exposed right flank much as it had done under its beloved commander two months ago at Chancellorsville—and, just as it had done two months ago, Howard's right crumbled under the weight of Johnson's two brigade front, two-brigade deep assault.

Early's division, meanwhile, had been placed in the rear (left echelon) of Johnson's men and began delivering the same type of flanking fire against the First Division of Slocum's corps as it emerged from the gap to support Howard's assault against Pickett's fortified position to their immediate front. The result was that panicked bluecoats either ran to their left spreading disorder among

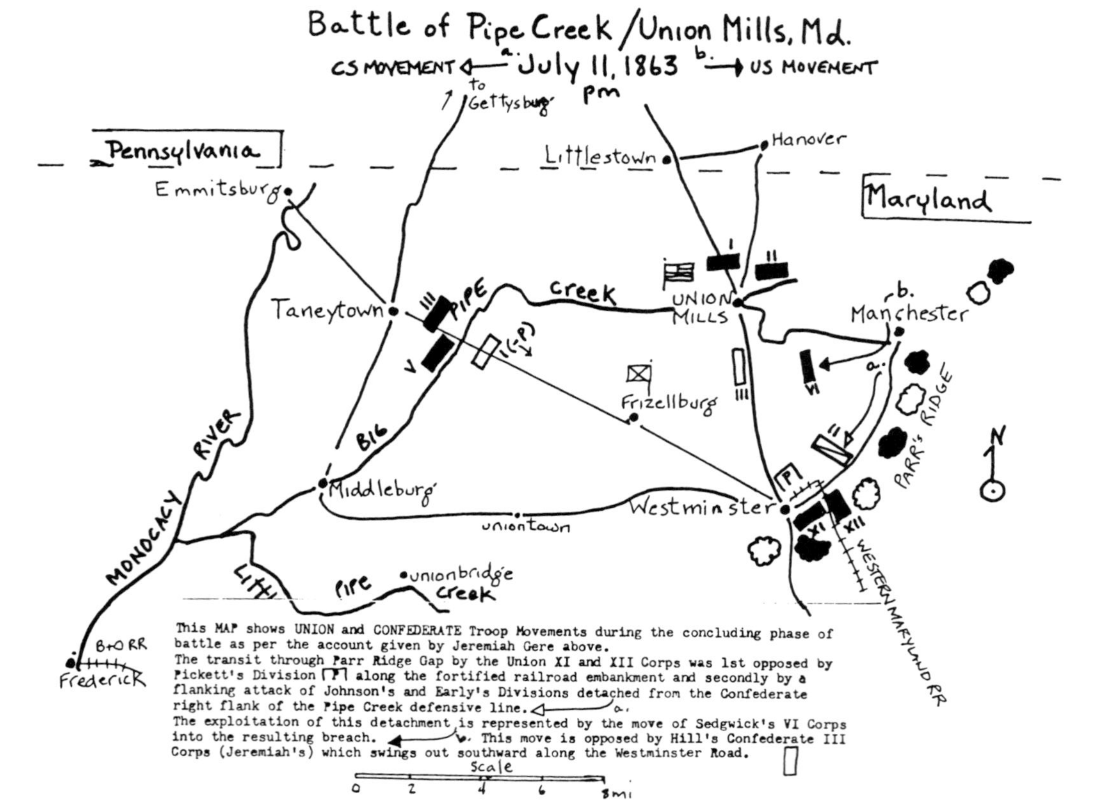

This MAP shows UNION and CONFEDERATE Troop Movements during the concluding phase of battle as per the account given by Jeremiah Gere above.
The transit through Parr Ridge Gap by the Union XI and III Corps was 1st opposed by Pickett's Division [P] along the fortified railroad embankment and secondly by a flanking attack of Johnson's and Early's Divisions detached from the Confederate right flank of the Pipe Creek defensive line. ← a.
The exploitation of this detachment is represented by the move of Sedgwick's VI Corps into the resulting breach. ← b. This move is opposed by Hill's Confederate III Corps (Jeremiah's) which swings out southward along the Westminster Road.

Scale
0   2   4   6   8mi

the troops in that direction, which retarded a necessary shift in their battle line to meet the Confederate assault, or else they tried to run back to the relative safety of the Parr Ridge Gap to their rear. This latter choice, however, exposed them to a withering fire from Early's overlapping left flank and many fell before reaching their destination.

Whether by chance or design, Slocum had placed his Second Division under Brigadier-General John Geary in the mouth of the gap where quickly-dug rifle pits and artillery emplacements provided a temporary haven and rallying point for those men and units that managed to escape the onslaught of General Lee's flanking attack. Needless to say, many prisoners were taken that afternoon down at Parr Ride Gap that became an impediment to our army's movement during the rest of the campaign. For now, however, the euphoria which began sweeping through the Army of Northern Virginia in the early afternoon of July 11, 1863, more than outweighed the stalemate it had experienced on July 2nd up at Gettysburg. In "Listening to Old Pete," General Lee had restored our army once again to its chosen mode of securing victory against superior numbers and resources. (See MAP p. 58).

Despite the euphoria raised by the recollection of specific events, there always seems to coexist a chapter in the life history of individuals and nations that acts as a counterpoint. If I had the ability to exercise such a chapter from this brief history of the role I played in the Army of Northern Virginia, the record would end here, omitting the fourth chapter in the Battle of Union Mills. Yet, the far larger purpose to be served in setting the record straight as to why our second northern incursion in ten months was thwarted, prevents me from doing this.

Indeed, if the account I provided thus far is to have

any integrity, I must prove it by admitting the bitter with the sweet. Suffice it to say that those accounts—written and verbal—which attribute our withdrawal from Pipe Creek to the turning of our right flank by General Meade are mistaken. It should be clear from my description of the third phase above that our "right" had already been detached from the line above the creek to plug the threat to our rear six miles distant by the transit of Howard's and Slocum's Corps through the Parr Ridge Gap. In a strict military sense, if military units (i.e., the divisions of Johnson and Early) are not on the field of battle, it is tactically incorrect to say they were defeated in that battle. Further, as far as the number of men engaged, taken prisoner and killed, the fight down at Parr Ridge Gap on July 11, 1863 might stand as a separate battle to the glory of Johnson's and Early's division, rather than an unfounded charge that they were caught unaware and flatfooted by the sudden arrival of Sedgwick's Sixth Corps on the right of our works overlooking Pipe Creek.

Suffice it to say that the railroad was not the only technology brought up to our rear by the Yankee XI and XII Corps that fateful day. When Slocum witnessed the awesome assault thrown against the right flank of these attacking columns down by the gap, the telegraphers in his signal corps relayed the news back up the tracks of the Western Maryland to the town of Manchester, which we earlier judged to be free from Yankees. In the main, this had been an accurate assessment and one which allowed General Lee to choose the units he did for his flanking assault down at the gap. In actuality, Sedgwick, either through his own initiative or through later orders from Meade, had chosen to guard the Union left by placing his Corps at a right angle to Pipe Creek rather than parallel to it. This disposition withdrew his entire corps from the sight of Ewell's men who could only see to the first hill-top north of Pipe Creek and not beyond it.

Sedgwick, subsequently, had patrolled the two-mile space between his east-facing front and Manchester by light cavalry patrols and—what proved to be our undoing—by placing a telegraphy unit in the town to keep Meade apprised of the whereabouts of Howard's and Slocum's Corps coming up the tracks from the south. When Meade learned from Slocum that identifiable units from our Second Corps (i.e., the Stonewall Brigade) were engaged to the rear, he ordered Sedgwick to move up to our now-defenseless right and, once gaining the heights, turn his three divisions west, attacking our line from that direction.

Needless to say, we had to abandon our north-facing trenches on the double to meet Sedgwick's assault coming from the east. Rodes's men were already running westward under the initial shock of so many bluecoats appearing suddenly to their right and we tried to grab the slower ones as they streamed through our new line now being formed at a right angle to the old along the west side of the Union Mills-Westminster Road. As our division swung out at this right angle to our old trench line, however, it became exposed to a renewed cannonade from the Yankee batteries down at Union Mills. Shots which had been largely ineffective when we were under the shelter of our trench were now traversing the length of our ranks with fearful effect.

I swear that when Sedgwick's first volley hit our new front, a lot of us were almost tempted to follow Rodes's men to the new rear if it had not been for a red beacon, which suddenly appeared down the road to our right. "Old Baldy" himself, now stripped to his red fighting shirt, was waving us to him like a person directing a picnic game of "snatch the bacon." "Form on me, boys, form on me," I remember him calling. "Pender will back you!" Apparently, that's all we University Grays needed to hear, for we raced toward our Third Corps Commander forming the extreme right of our new line along the Westminster Road.

We began firing by-the-nines right quick and of all the battles I was a party to, I was most sure on July 11, 1863 at Union Mills, Maryland, that each of my shots was causing a casualty because my unit was firing into a veritable ocean of blue coming over the heights toward us. The noise was deafening and by the feel of my Enfield's barrel, I knew yours truly was contributing significantly to the volume. My last rational recollection of this battle was that General Hill had galloped off shouting something about Pender's division while leaving a few of his staff officers behind our firing line. The sound of his horses's hooves were still discernable to me when it seemed that a bolt of lightning struck the front of my muzzle traveling down it and into my left side. All else became as a sudden rushing of wind cascading over me. I could not stand against it despite the urgent message sent to my legs. A sudden shock to my knees as I hit the ground indicated I was still conscious and a part of this world, but, again, my entire body felt dead to what my mind was willing it to do. Then I became aware of a force outside of my body pulling me upward, despite the onrushing wind, which was getting louder and more monotonal.

Shortly, I felt myself moving forward and in an upward-downward motion all at the same time. Through the heartstopping fear of being in such a strange state, coupled with an unmanly desire to surrender breath to the suffocating rush of that inhuman wind, there came a familiar voice—a voice from my boyhood, reassuringly firm and gentle at the same time. I could not identify the speaker then, but the things spoken about conjured up the most vivid images; the gentle rolling hills at Oxford, metaphors from the literary masterpieces I had studied, moonlight falling on the auburn hair of my first love, the strains of music emanating from our graduation cotillion. Like a palliative, the vividness of these images seemed to break through the harsh wind that had engulfed me to calm my psyche with the conviction that I would survive.

My return to full consciousness took place twelve days later (July 14th) in a hospital tent south of the Rapidan. It was there that Dr. Holt told me of the successful extrication of our army from the Pipe Creek Line and how I was brought to him. It seems that shortly after I was hit, General Hill had struck the extreme left flank of Sedgwick's attacking corps with Pender's division. This had caused the attack to stall and shift to the south of west to meet this new threat. This shift, however, had exposed the Yankee rear to a "blind" cannonade coming from Union Mills in support of Doubleday and Hays who were preparing to move up against our now-empty trenches.

Meanwhile, following General Lee's orders to his Corps Commanders to withdraw toward his headquarters at Frizelburg, Old Pete released Hood's Division on the way down to support a counterattack against Sedgwick's right front, which had the effect of driving him back to the shelter of our old breastworks. From Frizelburg, Maryland, the Army of Northern Virginia, now sorely pressed from three sides, withdrew southwest through Uniontown and across Little Pipe Creek at Union Bridge. Early's and Johnson's Divisions rejoined what was left of Rodes's division at the former place, having passed safely behind Pickett's fortified position down at

Parr's Gap. After abandoning this position during the night of July 12th, 1863, Pickett's division rejoined its First Corps comrades at the town of LIBERTY, Maryland.

My personal extrication from the Pipe Creek Line is of less importance to the historical record, but no less miraculous in the telling. It seems I was deposited at Dr. Holt's field hospital by a major riding a black horse with white stockings. "Save him, Doctor. He is the last of our Grays," was all the officer had said, but from Dr. Holt's description, I have no doubts that my benefactor was none other than Billy Lowry. Now, thanks to him who created our company, the first to die in the historical record of Pickett's Charge has become—like Ismael—the last to survive the alternate road taken in "Listening to Old Pete" in the summer of '63.

Then and Now

For four long years I wore the gray
   And followed my old brigade
All over old Virginia
   On the Pennsylvania raid.
Came west with General Longstreet
   In eighteen sixty-three
And fought and starved with General Bragg
   In eastern Tennessee.
Our clothes grew old and faded,
   And sad indeed our plight,
But we plodded on in rags and hope
   Believing we were right.
We used to hate the "bluecoats"
   And all the Yankee crew,
Our souls were wrapped in Dixie,
   We fought and cussed the blue.
I never dreamed in those old days
   That I would live to see
The sons of comrades wear the blue
   Who marched and fought with Lee.
But time, they say, will mellow wine,
   It mellows passions too,
For I was proud to see my son
   Go marching off in blue.

—Anonymous[13]

Part II

Four

"... it seems to me that the elan of the southern soldier was never seen after Chickamauga—that brilliant dash which had distinguished him was gone forever."

—D.H. Hill

In July 1863, having failed to achieve the far greater consequences of replicating the battle of Fredericksburg on the banks of Pipe Creek, Maryland, the First Corps of the Army of Northern Virginia returned to the familiar fields around Fredericksburg, Virginia, for rest and recuperation. Many veterans found themselves on guard duty or billeted on the exact spot they had occupied during that quintessential Confederate victory seven months ago. Most talked of how so little had changed in the interim—the remains of Yankee bridge-building, the skeletons of disabled caissons, the gutted buildings in the town. One enlisted man in the Fourth Texas Regiment would wax poetic in later years about an oil painting that still inspired his imagination as it hung in a bombed-out sniper's nest down by the Rappanhannock. Ironically, the subtitle of this painting, "Watching and Waiting," was an all-too-accurate description of what the Southern soldier could no longer afford to do as autumn 1863 approached.

On August 15, 1863, the young Texan's Corps Commander wrote to Secretary of War Sedden as to why the "dispersed defensive" strategy of Southern armies must be abandoned if hope for Southern Independence was to be kept alive. This failed strategy, he wrote, had left Joe Johnston's army in Jackson, Mississippi, "watching and waiting" for Grant's victorious force to move from Vicksburg; it had left Braxton Bragg's Army of Tennessee "watching and waiting" for Rosecrans to move against Chattanooga, and it had Lee's Army of Northern Virginia "watching and waiting" for Meade to move against the Rapidan. In short, wrote Lieutenant General James Longstreet, it was time to consolidate the South's scattered forces and assume offensive operations at that place which would create the greatest benefit for the Cause. This offensive, Longstreet suggested—since Grant already possessed the "lungs" of the South—should be against Rosecrans, who was threatening the "heart" of the south at Chattanooga. A successful counterattack here would draw resources away from Grant and Meade to stem a Confederate tide that threatened to rise above the Ohio.[1]

The depiction of a Yankee victory at Chattanooga as a sword pointed at the Southern heartland, however, did not originate with "Old Pete's" letter to Sedden on August 15, 1863. The two men had discussed the necessity for a consolidated offensive against Rosecrans as early as May when Longstreet was passing through Richmond in a belated attempt to aid Lee at Chancellorsville. Indeed, there is sufficient historical evidence to show that Longstreet preferred a spring consolidation of Southern arms against Rosecrans rather than a summer invasion of Pennsylvania by the Army of Northern Virginia. It was Sedden's verbal admonition to keep him apprised of this alternative plan in May that allowed Longstreet to ignore the chain of command with his August letter. Although his contemporaries were more impressed with Longstreet as a battlefield tactician than as an overall strategist, support for the August letter came from superiors and subordinates alike. For instance, when Longstreet told Lee of his letter three days after dispatching it, Lee calmly recalled a similar discussion both men had after Chancellorsville and concluded by asking his "Old War Horse" if he would be willing to take his First Corps west "and take charge there."[2]

It is obvious from the correspondence between the two men after Lee reported to Richmond several days later, that President Davis himself had been allowed by Lee to view the consolidation plan in a favorable light.[3] This in spite of the fact that Lee personally was loathe to leave Virginia to command it, as both Longstreet and Davis wished. At the other end of the chain of command, Colonel E. F. Alexander, artillery chief of the First Corps, claimed that the plan for reinforming Bragg in front of Chattanooga should have been implemented before Lee's return from Gettysburg and condemned its "dilatory consideration and slow acceptance."[4] Nevertheless, as historian Glenn Tucker wrote in *Chickamauga—Bloody Battle in the West,*

> It is unlikely, except for Longstreet's suggestion, that the troop movement which was to give the Confederacy life and opportunity for an additional year and a-half, would have been undertaken.[5]

Subsequent events of the next few weeks vindicated both Alexander's and Longstreet's concern regarding immediacy in aiding Bragg. The original consolidation plan approved by Davis and Lee called for but two of Longstreet's divisions (Hood's and McLaws's) to be sent to

Chattanooga via the direct line of the Virginia and Tennessee Railroad, which ran through Knoxville—a two-day trip of 540 miles. With the capture of Knoxville by Burnside, however, the alternate route through the Carolinas and Augusta, Georgia, would require ten days to cover 925 miles.

It is appropriate here to describe another line that ran more directly from Richmond to the beleaguered Braxton Bragg. This line was invisible to the eye, but its terminus was indelibly engrafted onto the heart and mind of the Confederacy's President. In approving Longstreet's consolidation plan, Jefferson Davis was paying off a line of credit that stretched back to February 23, 1847 at a place called Buena Vista. Here, as the enraged legions of Santa Anna closed in on Colonel Davis's red-shirted Mississippi Regiment, he had offered up a desperate prayer to the Almighty as his last hope of salvation. Salvation came in the form of Braxton Bragg. Through the sudden thunderclap of Bragg's artillery barrage and the voluminous white clouds, which issued forth, the "ugliest man in the Corps" galloped past, sword in hand, to lead the counterattack that saved the day for the Americans and the life of the future President of the Confederacy.

Now, in September 1863, bereft by circumstances of a field command, Davis saw in Longstreet's plan a two-fold means of repaying a long-overdue personal debt as well as a means of breathing new life into the faltering dream of Southern Independence.[6] As these two objectives began their inevitable divergence after Chickamauga, the South's President would be forced to make an agonizing decision. On October 20, 1863, he would offer Bragg's command of the Army of Tennessee to Longstreet in hopes that a historical alternative to "watching and waiting" could recoup the last Confederate victory in the West.[7]

One of the first direct witnesses to the scope involved in Longstreet's consolidation strategy was Colonel Oates of the Fifteenth Alabama. In the vanguard of those First Corps troops to reach Atlanta, Oates and the rest of Law's Alabama Brigade were forced to wait an entire day as trainloads of Joe Johnston's troops rumbled northward out of Mississippi to reinforce Bragg. Meanwhile, abandoning Knoxville, Tennessee, Confederate Major General Simon Buckner was bringing his corps to join Bragg. Ironically, Burnside's capture of that city had served to strengthen Confederate consolidation around Chattanooga without aiding Rosecrans in the slightest. In addition, by September 13, 1863, it seemed most Northern leaders except Rosecrans had divined Longstreet's strategic objective.

From a Confederate deserter in northern Virginia, Meade's spies and Halleck's logical deductions, the United States War Department had finally concluded that a major alteration in the South's strategy of a "dispersed defensive" was under way. Bragg was being reinforced to assume the offensive against Rosecrans. The latter had been dead wrong in assuring President Lincoln that Grant could better contain Joe Johnston after the fall of Vicksburg. With Grant convalescing in New Orleans, the Federal army he had led now seemed powerless to contain the transfer of Johnston's men to the Tennessee Valley. Upon learning at Enterprise, Mississippi, that his brigade would move north, John T. Goodrich of Fayetteville, Tennessee, exalted, "With buoyant expectancy, we Tennesseans were hoping that General Bragg would be sufficiently reinforced to recover our state and that we might see our home folks again after an absence of nearly two years."[9]

Two days before Goodrich's departure from Mississippi, Longstreet described his leave-taking of Lee:

> As I left General Lee's tent, after bidding him goodbye, he walked out with me to my horse. As my foot was in the stirrup, he said again, "Now, General, you must beat those people out in the West." Withdrawing my foot to a respectful position, I promised, "If I live; but I could not give a single man of my command for a fruitless victory."[10]

Before leaving Richmond, however, Longstreet intimated to Lee what he would state more emphatically the closer he got to Bragg—that Marse Robert's presence was a sine qua non for Confederate success in the West, i.e., "All that we have to be proud of has been accomplished under your eye and under your orders." Later historians would concur that the consolidation strategy then evolving toward the Army of Tennessee had a chance only if Lee was commanding it. Some even assert that in not going West, as Longstreet and Davis had wished, Lee made "the greatest mistake of his career."[11] Certainly, history contains enough examples of how such strategic shifts reversed the fortunes of war, such as Washington's transfer of his army from the Hudson Highlands to the Yorktown Peninsula, trapping Cornwallis. As Glenn Tucker noted in . . . *Bloody Battle in the West:*

> Grant and Halleck too, were caught off guard. The splendid army with which Grant had taken Vicksburg had been broken up rather recklessly and assigned to side ventures. Grant himself was out of action lying incapacitated in a New Orleans hospital. For once the South could bring ample manpower to bear on a battlefield. If Rose-

crans could be hurled back to the Ohio River, most of the territory that had been lost by the south in two and a-half years of struggle could be regained. Lee, who ranked Bragg . . . would possess the audacity and intrinsic genius to wring the most from any battlefield victory.[12]

Yet such comments as the above go further in commending the wisdom of Longstreet's strategic initiative than in demonstrating Lee's unwillingness to implement it in person. Indeed, from a purely strategic viewpoint, if Lee refused to leave his "native" Virginia to command the armies of the United States in 1861, his refusal to leave Virginia to lead a consolidated offensive against Rosecrans in 1863 might be the second "mistake of his career." The historic record shows that the zenith of Southern arms was reached on September 20, 1863 when the attack columns of "Old Pete" smashed the Federal center in the dense thickets along Chickamauga Creek, making Rosecrans the only Union general in the Civil War to lose a battle to a superior number of Confederates.

At that point, Longstreet urged Bragg to do exactly what Lee would have commanded him to do—assume offensive operations north of the Tennessee River. Forced to choose between this sound tactical advice and his loyalty to Braxton Bragg, President Jefferson Davis himself ordered Bragg on October 12, 1863 to carry out Longstreet's suggestion for crossing the Tennessee River Bridge at Bridgeport, Alabama. Bragg's dilatory response to this order, and its consequences for the Army of Tennessee, will form the basis of our alternative analysis in part two of this study.

As for those latter-day strategists (and they are probably in the majority) who view Gettysburg and Vicksburg as twin nails in the coffin of Southern independence, Longstreet's strategy of a consolidated offensive two months later might seem a quixotic, even suicidal measure initiated by desperate men in the Confederate high command. To this belief, the personal account of a non-com who "came west with General Longstreet in 1863" provides an interesting counterpoint, i.e.,

> . . . success at Gettysburg was not a physical victory for Meade. The Confederates held every foot of ground they occupied when the battle began . . . Gettysburg was a drawn battle . . . when we pulled out, we made thousands of weary, worn-out Yankees supremely happy. They stood on Cemetery Ridge and Little Round Top and were so glad to see us go that they forgot to shoot . . . as we marched slowly from the field. A farewell salute was certainly due us on our departure, for we had made it extremely interesting for them. . . . We took all our paraphernalia off with us that was of any value, leaving only a few broken gun carriages, donating the old junk as souvenirs to the enemy.[13]

At the divisional level, Lafayette McLaws, who had commanded some of the toughest combat of the summer, penned his wife as his men boarded the trains to Chickamauga:

> The taking of Vicksburg will release our army and require the enemy devote a considerable force to holding the Mississippi. We are (to be) concentrated in the interior and are increasing daily in strength and efficiency . . . the old spirit of self-confidence.[14]

In addition to the confidence they felt boarding the trains at Louisa and Orange Court House on September

9th, Longstreet's battle-hardened veterans looked confident as well. Governor Zebulon Vance of North Carolina had dispatched 14,000 new uniforms directly to the First Corps from blockade runners recently arrived at Wilmington. The generosity of this gift was heightened by the fact that not one North Carolina soldier was going west under "Old Pete."

If the high command in Richmond had expressed confidence in Longstreet's plan for a consolidated offensive after Gettysburg and Vicksburg, the general populace along the route west sanctified it with their hearts. G. Moxley Sorrel, chief of staff for the First Corps, wrote how much more than just food and drink were brought to the trains at every depot throughout Virginia, the Carolinas and Georgia, i.e., "Kisses and tokens of love and admiration for these war-torn heroes were ungrudgingly passed around." Mary Boykin Chestnut, the reliable Southern diarist, married to the Governor of South Carolina, was in Kingsville when the miles of flatcars and boxcars passed and prayed, "God bless those gallant fellows" whose abstinence from profanity, alcohol, or rudeness became benchmarks of their eight-day journey.

In short, those legions of historians who are prone to analyze the demise of Southern hopes after July 4, 1863 would be wrong to view Longstreet's strategy as an act of desperate men—a last throw of the dice before cashing in. The fact was that the South itself had not given up hope for what Thomas Paine had described as a "drawn game" during America's first War for Independence. Certainly the condition of the Confederacy in September 1863 was not as desperate as the one faced by Washington in the depth of a Valley Forge winter. Indeed, like the British in the eighteenth century, the North was calculating the costs of subjugating its rebels—by 1863 it was taking two

Federal soldiers plus $100,000 to kill one Southern soldier. Many in the North were considering this cost too high as the trains of First Corps rumbled toward Bragg's Army of Tennessee in early September. At times, it seemed to both combatants that only Lincoln's resolve stood between continuing the war and granting self-determination to the South.[15]

Throughout the region now being traversed by Longstreet's expeditionary force, hope was still strong that a victory over Rosecrans's Army of the Cumberland could prove to be the coup d' grace that opened the road to eventual independence. An early indicator of the success of Longstreet's consolidation proposal occurred in the roll call of the Army of Tennessee when he reported to Bragg's headquarters at eleven P.M., September 19, 1863. Sixty-six thousand troops were now at the latter's disposal and less than twenty-four hours later, Major General William Rosecrans would earn the more long-term but considerably more dubious distinction of becoming the only Union General to be defeated by a numerically-superior Confederate force.[16]

Approaching Bragg's headquarters near Chickamaugua Creek, Longstreet and his staff had barely escaped capture by Federal pickets, by calling out "Friends" to their initial challenge. It did not take long after arriving at Bragg's tent for this delegation from the Army of Northern Virginia to realize that their new commander was as devoid of friends as he was of victories over the Federals.

Forced by an ambitious father to rise above the haughtiness of the planter class of Warrentown, North Carolina, by attending West Point, it was there that young Braxton earned the only superlative of his life—"Ugliest man in the Corps." The commander of the

Army of Tennessee was perhaps the only Southern boy who never mentioned his mother despite his life-long penchant for letter writing. What others knew about this woman, Bragg had spent a lifetime trying to forget, i.e., during her pregnancy, Margaret Crossland Bragg had been sentenced to jail for killing a free black for impertinence. One contemporary account, since disproved, was that Braxton Bragg had been born in jail. Although many Southern leaders had hard beginnings,

> Young Braxton Bragg had risen each day in a class-ridden town that never ceased to remind him, in all the myriad Southern ways the South is so capable of, that his people were plebeians, that his mother was an ex-jail bird, and that the lot were unfit associates for the more elevated and refined. Hate, envy and malice can slip into one's bones very early in such an environment. Add to that a bad stomach and the worst luck in Christendom and you have Braxton Bragg falling back to Chattanooga with boils on his behind in a driving rain.[17]

Added to such a psycho-social biography of Bragg, was his military reputation as a martinet. His dogged, unimaginative frontal assaults by men marching elbow-to-elbow, against the "Hornet's Nest" at Shiloh, had cost the South dearly in men and precious time in the initial repulse of Grant's men below Pittsburg Landing. Coupled with his sullen retreat from Mufreesboro (Stone's River) and the abandonment of his prepared defenses at Chattanooga, were the round-robin letters he circulated to subordinates seeking empathy, but which returned to his tent expressing condemnation. Fortunately for Bragg, but not for the cause of Southern Independence, the only friend he seemed to have left in this fall of '63 was the one who mattered most—the President of the Confederacy, Jefferson Davis.

There is little indication that the commander of the Army of Tennessee showed any visible sign of relief (much less pleasure) at the arrival of Longstreet and his two divisions. The former's renewed confidence at the meeting, however, can be deduced by the reorganization of his newly-bolstered force into two large "wings," with "Old Pete" assigned command of the left wing. (Lieutenant General Leonidas Polk was given command of the right wing.) As Longstreet left Bragg's tent around eleven-thirty P.M., he joined the numerous critics of his new commander,

> The written order giving the plan was issued on the 18th. In general terms, it was to cross the Chickamauga, strike the enemy's left and roll it back on his right by a wheel to the left so as to come in between the enemy and Chattanooga. The work had become so persistent and assiduous during part of the 18th, and the 19th, that General Rosecrans came to understand the plan as well as his adversary . . . and to arrange accordingly.[18]

The irony of Longstreet's criticism, which would be documented by future historians of Chickamauga, was that his success on September 20th was largely attributed to the fact that Rosecrans "came to understand the plan (i.e., to turn his left) and arrange(d) accordingly." Simply stated, the zenith of both Confederate arms and Longstreet's reputation were established precisely because Rosecrans overreacted to Bragg's obvious plan to turn the Union left at Chickamauga. The fateful intersection between Rosecrans's overreaction to Bragg's plan and Longstreet's alternative decision to strike the center of the Yankee line, would occur at eleven A.M. Sunday, September 20th, near the Brotherton family's cabin on the Lafayette Road.

If the success of any battle plan could be determined solely by the preparation that preceded its execution, the outcome of the clash at the Brotherton Farm had been determined before taps on September 19th. Rather than going to bed after leaving Bragg's tent, Longstreet insisted on inspecting his left "wing" command whose many units were unknown quantities to him. Noting that the seven hundred acres of the partially-cleared farm to his front provided a more immediate objective for a consolidated offensive than Bragg's "grand wheel" provided for, he inquired for residents of the neighborhood who were under his new command. Jim Brotherton would tell later how his brother, Tom, was roused from fitful rest via "Old Pete's" request.

> We was raised right here and knew every pig trail through these woods. Saturday night, as soon as he got here, the gineral sent for Tom (who) . . . sez to me: "It's a sorry lad that won't fight for his own home, Jim. Remember that tomorrow." Then he left me and was with the gineral all that night and the next day.[19]

With Tom Brotherton providing details, Longstreet scoured the immediate terrain of dense undergrowth and partially-cleared fields formulating his plan of advance along each side of the Brotherton Road. A newspaperman would ask sarcastically in later years how much the Confederate victory at Chickamauga "belongs to Longstreet, the General and how much to Tom Brotherton, the private?" In fairness, this newspaperman should have pointed out that Rosecrans too had sent out a scout of the

Brotherton fields, a Captain Sanford C. Kellogg, who would end his military career overcompensating for the misinformation he would feed his chief on September 20th. Kellogg became the official mapmaker at Chickamauga when it was dedicated as our nation's first military park twenty-seven years after Rosecrans's defeat.[20]

Rising early, Longstreet began forming the tactical alignment of his new command that reflected his larger strategic plan for a consolidated offensive against the Army of the Cumberland. Ignoring the broad frontal alignment that Bragg's "wheel" order had implied and which Polk's right wing had executed on September 18th and 19th—Cleburn's single division having occupied a mile-wide front—"Old Pete" massed his left wing command into a grand column of assault superior in weight and depth to anything Lee had planned for Pickett or anything Bragg had undertaken thus far at Chickamauga. Compressed into a mere half-mile front consisting of two brigades, the grand column of assault measured eleven brigades deep, lined up behind each other in the darkened woods east of the Lafayette Road—sixteen thousand men, five times the population of Chattanooga itself, coiled like a compressed spring to slam shut the gateway to the Deep South.[21]

At approximately 10:45 A.M. September 20th, both Bragg and Rosecrans dispatched short notes that would have a profound effect on the success of the assault column. Exasperated by the delay of Polk's right wing in initiating the grand "wheel" against Rosecrans's left, Bragg dispatched an order allowing his divisional commanders to attack the Federal line at will. Freed from any thoughts of insubordination toward his commander's original plan, Longstreet proclaimed, "the hour of battle . . . at hand." His star was in its ascendence and in minutes his lead brigade would be christened for all time "the Star Brigade of Chickamauga." How much each would owe their distinction to the future official mapmaker of Chickamauga National Military Park would not be divined as "Old Pete's" arm came down at 11:10 A.M.

Less than an hour before, Captain Sanford C. Kellogg had been dispatched by the commander of Rosecrans's center (Major General George Thomas) to plead for reinforcements to the left of the Brotherton Farm. At the same time, the Federal troops facing Longstreet's assault column were the two remaining brigades of Brigadier General Thomas Wood's division arrayed along the western edge of the Brotherton Farm. These troops were clearly visible to Kellogg as he galloped along the Glen Valley Road (see X on Map), but the thick woods obscured Brannan's division on their left from Kellogg's view. In short, there appeared, to the future mapmaker of Chickamauga National Military Park, to be a massive gap in the Federal line between Wood's division and the right flank of Reynold's Fourth Division troops out on the Lafayette Road.

Kellogg immediately reported this misperception to Rosecrans's headquarters at the Widow Glenn's house, as the third courier sent by Thomas that morning requesting reinforcements for the left of the Federal line. Coupled with his awareness of Bragg's original tactic on the 18th and 19th, Thomas's rapid-fire requests for reinforcements to the left and his belief that this officer "has to be reinforced by the entire army," Rosecrans—knowing his capable aide Brigadier General James Garfield to be "engaged in another matter"—allowed Major Frank Bond to write the fateful order that cleared the way for the Confederate grand assault.

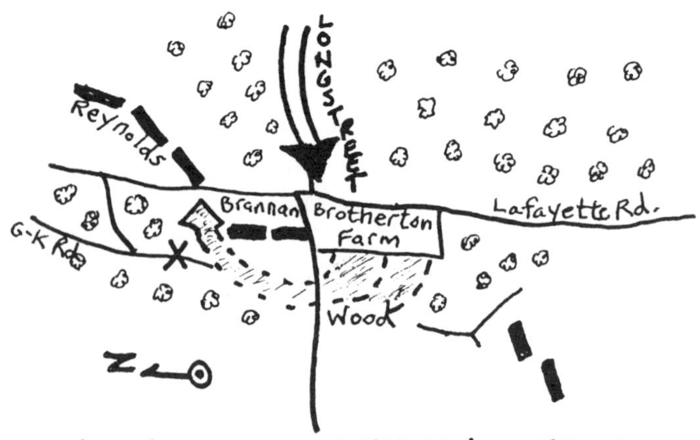

WOOD'S FATEFUL WITHDRAWAL FROM the BROTHERTON FARM TO SUPPORT REYNOLDS

Headquarters, Department of the Cumberland
September 20, 1863—10:45 A.M.
Brigadier General Wood, Commanding Division:

The general commanding directs that you close up on Reynolds as fast as possible and support him.
Respectfully,
Frank Bond, Major Aide d' Camp

At 10:55 A.M., fifteen minutes before Longstreet's attack, Wood started to move his brigades out of line opposite the Brotherton Farm. The fateful nature of the above order occasioned long and spirited debate even after the war was over. In light of our purpose to evaluate the effects of General Longstreet's alternatives against the historical record, these debate points are summarized below more as reasons for the success of his grand assault column than as an analysis of Federal defeat at Chicka-mauga. Certainly, if Bragg had adhered to his original battle plan, Wood's move could have resulted in a far different outcome.

1. Brigadier General Wood—"The order was not only mandatory, but peremptorily mandatory. It directed me to close up upon General Reynolds, a movement of one body from the rear to another body in front of it. It gave me the reason for the movement—viz., to support the body of troops in the front (left)—the most important reason that can exist on the field of battle."
2. Lieutenant General Rosecrans (via Whitelaw Reid)—"Even if a literal execution of the order had been possible, (Wood's) obedience to it approached criminality. He knew the enemy (Longstreet's column) was in his front, and also that Brannan was to his left."
3. Major General John Palmer—"The fault of the order was that it was not addressed to the (21st) Corps Commander, Crittenden, who by virtue of his rank had a wider latitude in modifying its execution than could Wood an 'unfortunate' division commander forced to obey an order dictated by ignorance of the situation."
4. John Clark Ridpath (Garfield's biographer)—"Had Garfield been consulted, that order would never have been written since he knew the position of every division on the field and that no gap existed between Wood and Reynolds."

Despite the volume of controversy that would swirl around the high point of Confederate arms in the West, most agree that Wood began executing the fateful order from Rosecrans's aid fifteen minutes before Longstreet's assault column poured across the Lafeyette Road and into the cleared fields of the Brotherton Farm. The diagram below[22] only hints at the coincidental timing that any movie director of the battle's reenactment could envy.

"We started on the run," said Elijah Wiseman of the seventeenth Tennessee, "and raised the rebel yell." Like a torrent, the vanguard of the grand assault column under Bushrod Johnson smashed into and surged over a strong Federal skirmish line behind the Brotherton's fence. Entering the cleared fields, the angle of Federal fire from right and left indicated the fateful gap left by Wood's departure from the center fifteen minutes earlier.

Like a flash flood, the assault column flowed into the

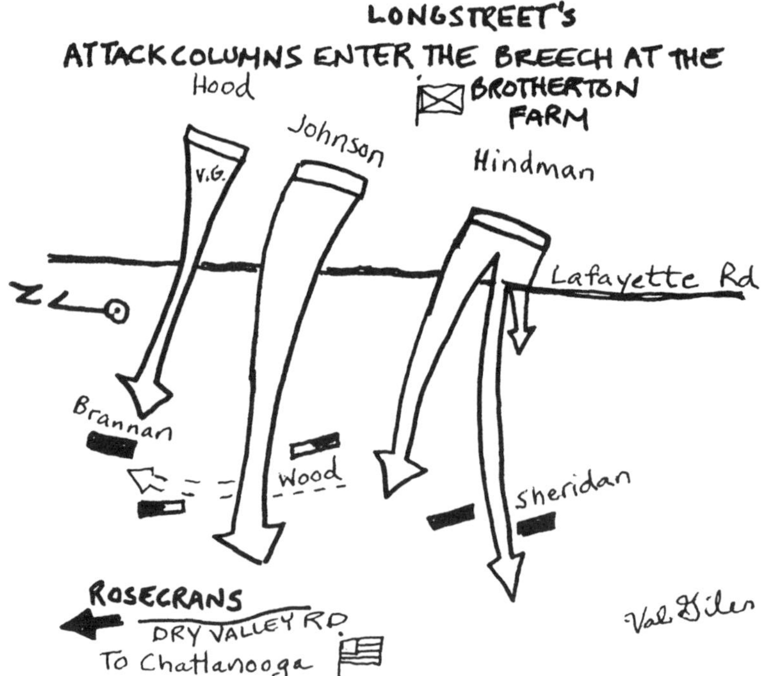

gap, flinging aside like driftwood the blueclad units of
Davis and Beaumont, who tried to stem the tide from
their positions north and south of the opening. Eventually, this gray and butternut tide smashed into the rear
elements of Wood's Division, which had been poking
along toward what they thought would be a supporting
role for Reynolds out on the Lafayette Road to the north.
The torrent, hitting Wood's column at right angles, cap-
sized the order of march, spewing bluecoats in every direction of the compass except east. Finally emerging from
a second line of darkened forest, the Confederate vanguard beheld the outline of Missionary Ridge rising majestically against an azure sky. The feeling of having
reached some apotheosis was captured in Bushrod Johnson's battle report:

> The scene now presented was unspeakably grand. The
> resolute and impetuous charge, the rush of our heavy col-
> umns sweeping out from the shadow of gloom of the forest
> into the open fields flooded with sunlight, the glitter of
> arms, the onward dash of artillery and mounted men, the
> retreat of the foe, the shout of hosts of our army, the dust,
> the smoke, the noise of firearms—of whistling balls and
> grapeshot and bursting shell—made up a battle scene of
> unsurpassed grandeur.[23]

Almost sensing that the "grandeur" of the initial assault would give pause to his attack column, Longstreet
dispatched John B. Hood, his left arm in a sling and his
time left on the field measured in the minutes it would
take a mine ball to shatter his thigh. "Go ahead and keep
ahead of everything," the Texan urged Johnson. So on
Johnson pushed with Major General Hindman's division
on his left. Where Johnson encountered a Federal brigade, however, Hindman ran into two divisions. At a later

inquiry on the result, a Federal colonel would testify, "McCook's Corps was wiped off the field without any attempt at real resistance."

The witness went on report that officers and artillery, in seeking the rear first, had spread panic like a contagion among the infantrymen who were expected to remain behind manning flimsy barricades. Where the first group had fled the long gray column that had emerged howling from the dense woods, the latter had subsequently panicked at seeing so much gold braid and heavy artillery leaving them to go it alone. Phil Sheridan, whose fame would have to wait for later days, had been crossing behind McCook's lines under Rosecrans's original order to reinforce Thomas to the north, when the backflow of retreating bluecoats hit his two brigades broadside. Sheridan could think of nothing and fell into a laconic state that seemed to characterize almost the entire Federal officer corps as noon of September 20, 1863 approached, i.e.,

His spirit merely said that he should flee to fight and love and eat another day—for all living things want to live. It was not a unique situation. If your breastworks fail, if your defensive line breaks, if your men are flying backward under a mighty wave of gray, you haven't got time to pull out a map, suck on a pipe and try to figure what Wellington or Napoleon might have done . . . backpedaling men swept over those of Sheridan . . . a knot of humanity reeling backward. The day was done![24]

To Hindman's right, Johnson's men had reached Dry Valley Road where their commander halted them for a breather. Federals were swarming in disarray and, if Johnson had had a powerful pair of binoculars, he might have seen that their fleeing commander had also paused momentarily at a fork in the road down in the valley. The northwest fork led back to Chattanooga, away from the battle; the other ran east and then south to where General Thomas was about to make the stand that would be his life's defining moment. After a brief discussion with his aide, the future president, James Garfield, as to who should organize the defense of the city as opposed to the battlefield, Rosecrans turned northwest toward oblivion. An aide recalled the immediate effect of this decision on his commander's psyche upon reaching headquarters in Chattanooga: "The officers who helped him into the house did not forget the terrible look of a brave man stunned by sudden calamity. In later years, I used to occasionally meet Rosecrans, and always felt that I could see the shadow of Chickamauga upon his noble face."

As Rosecrans turned his eyes to the Almighty for guidance, Charles Dana, unofficial informant to Secretary of War Stanton, turned to the telegraph to apprise Washington of the defeat in the woods and fields of the Brotherton Farm.

My report today is of deplorable importance. Chickamauga is as fatal a name in our history as Bull Run. They came through with resistless impulse, composed of brigades formed in division. Before them our soldiers turned and fled. It was wholesale panic. Vain were all attempts to rally them. Our wounded are all left behind ... the total of killed, wounded and prisoners can hardly be less than 20,000.[25]

The irony of Dana's telegraphed message was that Washington would know of Bragg's victory before Bragg did. Southern accounts of the battle, running from generals to privates, describe their commander's physical and psychological detachment from what current terminology would call the "situation on the ground." Longstreet was certain that Bragg had heard around 5:30 P.M. the "voice of victory that joined in a tremendous swell of heroic harmony that lifted from their roots the great trees of the forest," as Thomas was finally dislodged from Snodgrass Hill.

Bragg apparently did not hear this sound and perhaps a dispatch from Longstreet would have been in order. Nonetheless, General Polk, perhaps feeling guilty over his delayed attack on Rosecrans' left, rode to Bragg's tent and reported the victory in person, but Bragg was not in a mood to hear good news from Polk, whom he was about to dismiss from command. According to an aide who was present when Bragg was awakened a second time in two nights, Polk reported, "the enemy was routed and fleeing precipitately from the field and that there was the opportunity to finish the work by the capture or destruction of Rosecrans's army, by prompt pursuit, before he had time to reorganize and throw up defenses at Chattanooga." Two days later when Polk was suspended, he would write the first of the post-Chickamauga letters to President Davis:

> The troops at the close of the fight were in the very highest spirits, ready for any service. . . . General Bragg did not know what happened. He let us down as usual and allowed the fruits of the great but sanguinary victory to pass from him by the most criminal negligence or rather incapacity.[26]

Polk probably never knew that hours after leaving Bragg, an escaped Confederate private had been brought to the latter's tent verifying the above assessment. The private reported Rosecrans's army in full retreat, leaving wounded behind in Chattanooga. Bragg, still incredulous (and not a little sleepy), asked the private if he even knew what a retreat looked like. The classic response, embellished by Confederate veterans down through the years at reunion halls and bivouacs, was reportedly: "I ought to, General. I've been with you during your whole campaign."

Whether the private's quip motivated Bragg to mount and seek out Longstreet the next morning is not clear, but it was the first time he appeared on the battlefield since Old Pete's assault column had surged forward the previous morning. According to Longstreet, Bragg asked his "views of the next step to be taken."[27] The reply was recalled in the former's autobiography:

> I suggested we cross the Tennessee River north of Chattanooga and march against the line of the enemy's rear; that if, after so threatening as to throw General Rosecrans's to full retreat, we found it inconvenient to pursue . . . we turn back with part of the army and . . . disperse the Union army in east Tennessee (Burnside's).[28]

Bragg left Longstreet around 6:30 A.M., September 21st with the understanding that this was to be the next step for the Army of Tennessee, and yet Forrest, who had already pursued the retreating Federals, was reined in several hours later when he gave a report favoring just such a move. "What does he fight battles for?" the outraged Forrest asked as he stomped from Bragg's tent.

Having been ordered to move forward after the right wing (whose former commander was now reading Bragg's suspension notice) and to care for the dead and wounded, Longstreet's command passed Bragg's new headquarters on the 22nd. Being directed here to detach a division from his column to follow the Federal route into Chattanooga, Longstreet asked if his original suggestion of crossing north of the city was to be abandoned. Bragg,

> . . . said the people would be greatly gratified to know that his army was marching through the streets of Chattanooga with bands of music and salutations of the soldiers.

Longstreet pointed out that the few people still left in Chattanooga would be far more elated if the Southern army passed over the Tennessee River first and forced the Federals from the city because the latter knew it couldn't be held without their supply line north of the river. Regrettably, however, Longstreet was forced to conclude that

> The praise of the inhabitants of a city so recently abandoned to the enemy, and a parade through its streets with bands of music and fluttering banners were more alluring to a spirit eager for applause than was the tedious march for fruition of our heavy labors.[29]

In the two days it took Braxton Bragg to move his victorious army the twelve miles separating the Chickamauga battlefield and the heights of Missionary Ridge, he had solidified his hold as the most despised general in the Confederacy. As a letter from a soldier named John W. Harris expressed it, "Everyone here curses Bragg, and if he is removed, it will put our troops in much better spirits." Such an assessment pales in comparison to that of Nathan Bedford Forrest when he learned that his cavalry corps that had led the pursuit of the Federals into Chattanooga, was to be placed under Joe Wheeler. According to

Forrest's chief surgeon, Dr. J. B. Cowan, Forrest rushed into Bragg's tent, brushing aside salutes and handshakes to jab his finger into his commander's face proclaiming,

> You have played the part of a damned scoundrel and are a coward, and if you were any part of a man, I would slap your face and force you to resent it. You might as well not issue any orders to me, for I will not obey them . . . and I say to you that if you ever again try to interfere with me or cross my path, it will be at the peril of your life.

In Bragg's defense, Forrest's outburst was insubordinate. It would be a carbon copy of the dressing down he gave later to another superior, John B. Hood, at Franklin, Tennessee. The so-called "frontier code" of not letting a personal affront pass without seeking satisfaction was an anathema to the success of any collective effort much less the destruction of an invading army. Certainly the depth of anger coursing through the ranks of the Army of Tennessee against its commander after Chickamauga was a simple reaction to the complete victory it had sensed when its divergent wings came together on Snodgrass Hill in the afterglow of September 20, 1863. It's axiomatic that the higher our hopes fly, the further they have to fall, yet a great part of Bragg's behavior rested on hard statistical and logical reasons for discontinuing the attack against Rosecrans's army, i.e.,

1. Southern losses were staggering, with Longstreet alone losing 8,632 of the 22,885 men committed to the attack on the 20th.
2. Many survivors of the initial attack were exhausted by their efforts at the Brotherton Farm and Snodgrass Hill as per the testimony of a soldier in Hood's Division that "we were fagged out after 48 hours of fighting."

3. Few of the artillery batteries used had not been immobilized by the loss of horses. One of the Brothertons noted that these animals were lying "everywhere" when he returned to check on his family after the battle.
4. The army's proximity to the railroad at Chickamauga station was needed for re-supply and evacuation of the wounded.

It is also axiomatic, however, that a body in motion tends to stay in motion, while a body at rest tends to stay at rest. As Bragg's decision to besiege Chattanooga and await an act of nature to starve the Federals out became known to his officer corps, a series of letters and meetings were initiated, which questioned Bragg's fitness for command. Although Longstreet initiated the first of such meetings on October 4, 1863, he resisted the suggestion that he should author a letter to President Davis. Citing protocol, "Old Pete" showed a greater willingness to communicate with Secretary of War Sedden, with whom he had initially proposed the concept of a "consolidated offensive" against Rosecrans. Subsequent deliberations eventually overrode this moderate position, however, and D.H. Hill wound up authoring a round-robin letter to the President, detailing reasons why Bragg should be sent elsewhere, citing his health rather than his courage. On October 9, 1863, President Davis arrived at Bragg's headquarters to conduct the strangest of three meetings dealing with alternatives to what the historical record would refer to as the siege of Chattanooga. Sandwiching in a private meeting with Longstreet on October 10th, the President would hold a last, collective meeting with the officer corps on the 12th before returning to Richmond.

The format chosen by President Davis for the evening meeting of October 9th would be tantamount to waving a red flag in a room of angry bulls. As the increasing besieged Bragg was ushered to a seat in the middle of his critical subordinates, Davis, after a few agonizing preliminaries, laid it bluntly on the line: "What did the subordinates think of their commander?" (Here, a question akin to a twentieth-century adage might have crossed Bragg's mind: "With friends like Davis, who needed enemies?") The President turned and faced Longstreet, who recalled later that "it seemed rather a stretch of authority even for a President and I gave an evasive answer and made an effort to turn the channel of thought, but he would not be satisfied and got back to his question." After referring briefly to the condition of the army, Longstreet concluded demurely that Bragg could be of greater service elsewhere than as its head. Apparently this set the tone for the other generals (Buckner, Cheatham, Hill), for they answered in kind, with Hill adding a little more relish as author of the letter Davis had received.

The meeting of October 9th dissolved without any positive results.

Early the following day, Davis appeared at Longstreet's tent and the two went for a walk that most sources refer to as a "private meeting," which lasted all day. According to Old Pete's *From Manassas to Appomattox,* he was offered command of the Army of Tennessee, but refused because "the time had passed for handling that army as an independent force." With the momentum of Chickamauga lost and the army entangled in a quasi-siege from Lookout Valley to Orchard Knob, the morale of officers and men had fallen into a trough. Meanwhile, Longstreet asserted, it had become evident to all, except Bragg, that Union armies were moving to reinforce Rosecrans from Mississippi and northern Virginia.

Again, Longstreet pushed the President to meet this renewed threat with a second consolidation through a redeployment of the army with Joseph Johnston's command in Alabama and Mississippi. The mention of Johnston's name, however, brought a rebuke from Davis, who launched into a tirade about the political pressures he was forced to endure as President of the Confederacy. Longstreet concludes his account of this meeting by recalling the words that "restored (Davis) to his usual, gracious calm: All the people asked for was success; with that the talk of politicians would be as spiders' webs before you." Nonetheless, the mutual mood for both men as this meeting ended was "akin to the clouds gathering about headquarters . . . faster than those that told the doom of the southern cause."[30]

For our purpose of analyzing a historical alternative to the "doom," which eventually befell Bragg's Army of Tennessee on November 25, 1863, President Davis's last meeting with its officer corps on October 12th is the critical one. At this meeting, the President of the Confederacy expressed his desire to pull the army out of its siege lines around Chattanooga and commit it to active duty in the field, calling "for suggestions and plans by which that could be done," and inviting Longstreet to speak first. In "Listening to Old Pete," the President of the Confederacy, who was both the commander-in-chief of Southern armies and Bragg's closest friend, chose the following alternative to a static siege that had robbed the momentum from the major Confederates army in the west:

I suggested a change of base . . . a march of the army to the railroad bridges of the Tennessee River at Bridgeport, (AL) and the crossing of the river as an easy move—one that would cut the enemy's rearward line, interrupt his supply train, put us between his army at Chattanooga and the reinforcements moving to join him, and force him to precipitate battle or retreat.[31]

Speaking next, Bragg obviously astounded Longstreet by proposing the exact plan he had rejected on the morning of September 21st when the latter had first proposed it: driving the Federals from Chattanooga by crossing the river north of town and swinging back to destroy his rear supply lines. Maps and arguments for each plan (both of them Longstreet alternatives to a siege) were presented to Davis and the meeting of October 12th concluded "When the President ordered the move to be made by the change of base."[32] Subsequent situation reports by Rosecrans made public after the war, described a Federal army rapidly depleting its rations for man and beast along with the conviction of its commander that needed reinforcements must hazard the torrential fall rains if the Army of the Cumberland were to survive. All this, wrote Longstreet,

> suggests that the campaign ordered by the President . . . could have forced him from his works in crippled condition and given us comfortable operations between him and his reinforcements coming from Virginia and Mississippi.[33]

Unfortunately for the South, the same mid-October rains that muddied the roads for Rosecrans's reinforcements, were the same rains that muddied the resolve of Braxton Bragg in carrying out President Davis's order for the redeployment of his army. It is doubtful, however, that given our alternative need to follow Old Pete to Bridgeport, Alabama, that Bragg would have considered it wise to totally disregard his President's order of October 12, 1863. In light of Bragg's life-long obsession to "go by the book," his singular fifteen-year, fire-forged friendship with Jefferson Davis and his more immediate desire to rid himself of all who disagreed with him, a partial detachment of Longstreet's command from Chattanooga can safely be deduced especially since it had more to recommend it than the later abortive detachment of Longstreet toward Knoxville as described in the historical record. The most obvious form such an order would take would be the following:

Headquarters, Army of the Tennessee
Missionary Ridge, October 15, 1863

To Lieutenant General James Longstreet,

Pursuant to the orders of the President, your command will proceed as soon as practicable to seize the bridge and rail center at Bridgeport, Alabama. The purpose of this mission is twofold:

1. To deny the enemy to our immediate front his nearest center of supply.
2. To interpose your force between him and any reinforcements moving to his relief from the west.

Braxton Bragg, Lieutenant General
Commanding, Army of the Tennessee

Five

"Shall we bury these men by their respective states, Sir?"
"No! Mix them all together—I'm tired of States' Rights."

> —General George Thomas
> "Rock of Chickamauga"
> Army of the Cumberland

My name is Valerius Cincinnatus Giles, currently second sergeant in the Fourth Texas Regiment, Robertson's Brigade, Hood's Division of Longstreet's Corps. Yes, I was one of these "graybacks" who came west with Old Pete in 1863 to fight and starve with General Bragg in eastern Tennessee near where I was born twenty-one years before. Both my name and eventual removal to Texas can be attributed to my father's fond preference for classical Roman history. Even the family dogs wound up with names like Caesar, Cassius, and Brutus, although I made it clear from early on that I was to be addressed as "Val" by anyone desirous of holding a peaceable conversation with me. About the time of my seventh birthday, Texas was finally relinquished by Mexico and Father, perhaps imbued with his own version of a "Pax Americana," removed us all to Austin where our descendants still reside.

These descendants are an important factor in answering the question as to why I was the one selected to give this firsthand account of General Longstreet's alternative to Bragg's protracted siege of Chattanooga. After all, there were over 5,000 of us First Corps veterans who boarded the trains at Guinea Station, Virginia, to carry out the "consolidated offensive" against Rosecrans. Like many, I kept a diary and wrote home prodigiously both before and after the Gettysburg incursion of Lee's army. These letters and diary entries were compiled by me after the war under the title, "Rambling Recollections of the Stormy Sixties," which appeared in serialized version in several Texas newspapers. Without an old family friend named Mary Laswell, however, my rambling might have wound up like so many others, which faded away in forgotten attic corners as their authors answered the last drumroll. Thanks to my family's long association with the Laswells, however,—Mary was the great granddaughter of my brother's Texas Ranger commander, Colonel Lubbock—my accounts of what American History would label variously as "the turning point of the Civil War" and "the high water mark of the Confederacy" would survive to this day. That such a history ends ingloriously for the Southern Cause, can be attributed, I believe, to the divisiveness that swept the Army of Tennessee after Bragg failed to maintain General Longstreet's initiative after Chickamauga.[1]

It is precisely this inglorious ending to my memoirs which has imbued me with a burning desire to "follow my old brigade" to Bridgeport, Alabama, in compliance with our President's order to Bragg on October 12, 1863. Jefferson Davis was singularly Bragg's closest friend and superior as our momentum brought us to the heights of Missionary Ridge during the autumn of our Confederacy's career. In "Listening to Old Pete," the President was convinced that this momentum should not be dissipated in a protracted siege of Chattanooga. Death in battle is not the most inglorious fate that can befall a soldier, whether general or private. I am convinced that my inglorious wind-up as a prisoner at Camp Morton, Indiana, was sealed when Bragg decided to ignore the President's Bridgeport order of October 12, 1863. In support of this conviction, I offer to the reader of these recollections my account of one night at Wauhatchie Station.

In retrospect, the Battle of Wauhatchie Station during the night of October 28, 1863 was a microcosm of all those negative factors that were converging in the fall of '63 to spell the doom of Confederate arms in the west. I won't even count among these the sullen, introspective pessimism of General Bragg that in one week had transmuted our collective euphoria over the success of Old Pete's grand assault at the Brotherton Farm into a morale-busting siege stretching six miles around the defeated Federals in Chattanooga. I'll leave any analysis of Braxton Bragg's behavior to posterity where it belongs. As a twenty-one-year-old infantryman in the Texas brigade, I'll simply list my observations on what I saw and felt at the time as to how the action at Wauhatchie represented the destruction of one of the most respected units ever enlisted in the Cause of Southern Independence.

First and foremost, this battle took place because Bragg failed to execute President Davis's October 12th order to seize the Federal supply center at Bridgeport, Alabama. Using this center as a jumping-off point two weeks later, General Hooker's force from the Army of the Potomac was able to invest Bragg's left in the Lookout Valley without any opposition whatsoever. (This despite the fact that our First Corps signal stations had reported on Hooker's progress along the south bank of the Tennessee River!) In all fairness, any accurate accounting of the action at Wauhatchie must include General Longstreet's reaction to Bragg's failure to launch a preemptive attack against Bridgeport. Our First Corps commander grew withdrawn and less cordial in his daily discourse, confessing in his memoirs of Wauhatchie, "it was an oversight of mine not to give definitive orders for the troops before leaving them." Thirdly, Federal success at Wauhatchie allowed completion of their famous "cracker line" from Bridgeport, which effectively broke our siege of Chattanooga. As General Grant telegraphed Washington after the battle, "The question of supplies may now be regarded as settled. . . . One week more and preparations may commence for offensive operations."[2]

It was common knowledge to both armies that Bridgeport, Alabama, was the major supply depot for the Yankees in Chattanooga. Since our First Corps held the extreme left of Bragg's siege line along Raccoon Mountain to Brown's Ferry, that supply depot was only one-day's march from our position along the south bank of the Tennessee River. Because of the peculiarities of the river, however, the Yankee supply route from Bridgeport stretched a full sixty miles along rough terrain on the north bank. This maddening reality for the Yankees was experienced firsthand by a crippled U.S. Grant who by October 23rd had been pushed and carried over the muddy, tenuous path into Chattanooga. In short, eleven days had elapsed between our President's order to seize Bridgeport and the arrival of the new Yankee commander whose first priority was to use reinforcements arriving in that town to shorten the "cracker line" vis-à-vis an attack on Bragg's left flank. One didn't have to be a life-long student of Napoleon to know that a preemptive attack against Bridgeport as recommended by General Longstreet and accepted by the President of the Confederacy would have wrecked havoc with Grant's plans and their subsequent execution by Hooker who strode up our side of the river to attack Bragg's left on October 28, 1863. (See Map p. 106.)

If the initiative of Chickamauga had been lost by Bragg's decision to lay siege to the defeated Yankees in Chattanooga, it is my belief that the siege of Chattanooga was lost when he failed to carry out the Bridgeport directive of October 12th. We learned afterward that Hooker was not acting alone in some gallant charge simply to alleviate Grant's pique at being carried into Chattanooga with his crutches. Such was not his nature and indeed his inept behavior at Chancellorsville five months before had cost him the support of most of Slocum's XII Corps except Geary's division, which was left at Wauhatchie Station as a rear guard to the action down at Brown's Ferry where we watched him proceed with Howard's XI Corps.

Even as these movements were being relayed to Bragg via observation posts stretching back towards Bridgeport, he refused to believe them to the point of rebuking members of our signal corps as he stood in conference with General Longstreet on the eastern slope of Lookout Mountain. Not to be deterred by all this gold braid, the last messenger reportedly told Bragg, "General, if you will ride to a point on the west side of the mountain, I will show them to you." At the sight of so many recently-arrived bluecoats in the valley below, it was reported by some that Bragg "fell into his usual snit, which caused Longstreet to become more sullen and removed . . . the more Bragg fumed, the more Longstreet resisted."[3] It was in such an atmosphere as this that the belated and ill-fated plan to attack Hooker's rear guard at Wauhatchie was conceived.

As I indicated above, Hooker was merely acting the

midwife to the brain-child conceived between Grant and "Old Baldy" Smith. Smith had sparked Grant with a plan to shorten the tortuous route to Bridgeport by breaking our weak grasp of Brown's Ferry with a daring amphibious operation on the night of October 27th. By seizing Brown's Ferry, a direct route across Moccasin Point would hasten supplies and manpower to the besieged Army of the Cumberland now commanded by General Thomas. The initial beachhead to be secured by a silent flotilla of about 1,400 men, however, would be too weak to hold once the Confederates discovered the plan. Enter Grant's order to Hooker to march east from Bridgeport with the XI (Howard's) and XII (Slocum's) Corps to secure and expand the Brown's Ferry beachhead.

At nine o'clock on the night of October 28, 1863, five weeks after our gallant charge at the Brotherton Farm, without bugle call or roll of drum, we were ordered to quietly fall in and off we moved westward like some silent band of Cherokees that had long ago intoned "Chatta" (crow) "nooga" (Nest) toward the sleepy settlement below. As a young non-com in Hood's famed Texas Division, I naively ascribed the isolation we felt that night to the absence of our famed commander whose severed right leg lay somewhere back in the deep thickets along Chickamauga Creek. After the war, I learned that the actual separation from my old command was occasioned by more insidious reasons that had begun to rend the cohesiveness of the First Corps even before its opening shots tore through the stillness surrounding Wauhatchie Station.

After a rapid march of several miles, we were formed in a battle-line on the crest of a hill, with our right falling short of the Tennessee River by about one hundred yards. This gap proved to be the undoing of our old brigade and the hard-won reputation of Hood's Division now commanded by Micah Jenkins. I later learned from Old Pete's memoirs that Jenkins had placed us in this untenable position simply to ally the complaints of Evander Law that he was too weak to block Hooker from rushing to the relief of the Yankee division (Geary's) left at Wauhatchie. Law's complaints, in turn, were fueled by additional matters of both heart and head that stretched back to Gettysburg. Evander Law had been Hood's immediate successor who had assumed command of the division when the latter was wounded at both Gettysburg and Chickamauga. When Jenkins was promoted above Law after the last battle, a deep resentment began to fester in the latter's heart long before we engaged Hooker's rear guard in the darkened gloom surrounding Wauhatchie. Tactically, Law knew something that even Longstreet did not know until he galloped down to our staging area from his command post up on Lookout Mountain—that Bragg had changed his mind about backing up our division with that of Lafayette McLaws. Hence, Old Pete's lament years later that "it was an oversight of mine not to give definitive orders for the troops to return to their camp before leaving them."

Well, Jenkins probably figured he couldn't fill Hood's boots by a "return to camp," so he decided to attack Geary's Division anyway with a severely-depleted force and no means of preventing Hooker from rushing to Geary's relief. If the political intrigue surrounding my last battle as a Confederate infantryman sounds convoluted, it should. There seemed to be a malaise that engulfed our First Corps from the moment Bragg halted its advance west of the Brotherton Farm. It was an infection that had never been a part of our service with the Army of Northern Virginia, but it was chronic enough to be still emanating from General Longstreet's memoirs when I opened

This Map shows the troop disposition during the action at Wauhatchie Station, TN on the
night of October 28-29, 1863 when Val Giles was captured: 1. General Hooker has brought
the XI and XII Corps into Lookout Valley from Bridgeport, AL. 2. Stationing Geary's
Division at Wauhatchie Station as a rear guard, 3. Hooker proceeds three miles down the
valley to enlarge the bridgehead at Brown's Ferry as ordered ▶ . 4. Longstreet's attack
against Geary is weakened when Bragg witholds McLaws' Division. 5. Jenkins (Hood's successor)
attacks Geary with a weakened division having stationed the brigades of Law and Robertson to
block any relief coming to Geary from Brown's Ferry. 6. Val Giles, a member of Robertson's
Brigade, is captured around 2am (x) when Hooker sends "German" relief columns against the
exposed right flanks of the "blocking brigades". 5

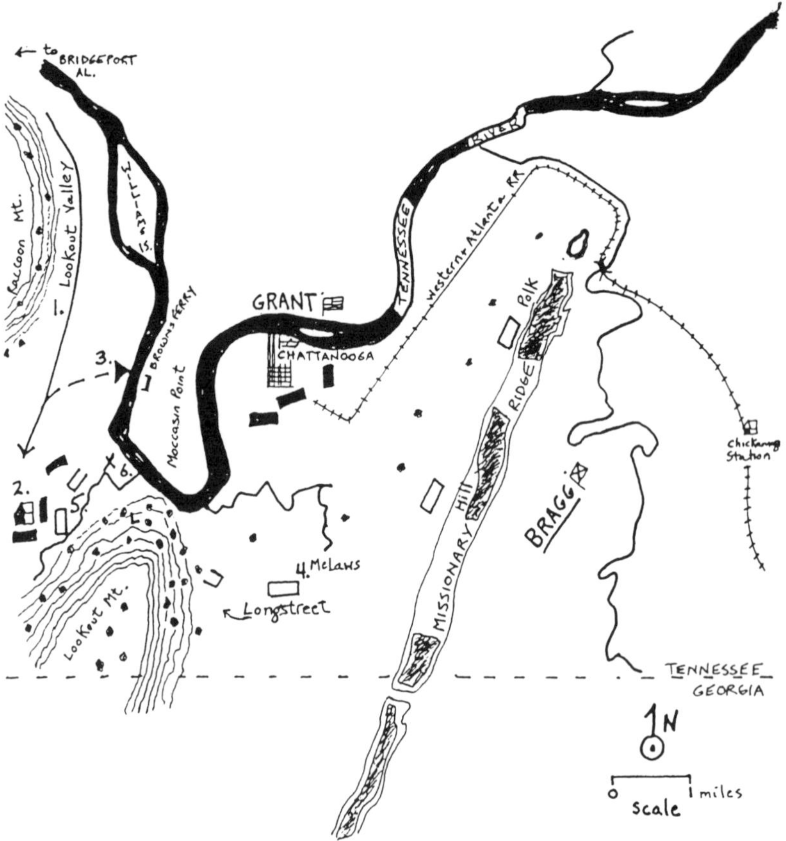

their pages twenty-five years after the war had ended. I had become convinced during that time that if we had taken the fight to Hooker at Bridgeport, as Old Pete had suggested, I could have stood with pride for the last roll at Appomattox.

The end for me as a rifleman in the Texas Brigade came about 2 A.M. on October 29, 1863 with our right dangling in the air and the crash of Jenkins's ill-fated attack going on to our left. It was then that we spied a strong line of bluecoats coming up against our exposed right flank with the gleam of their muskets and bayonets flashing in the frigid moonlight.

Colonel Bain, then in command of the Fourth Texas, ordered an orderly fall-back, but we began splitting underbrush and moonbeams wide open as we ran down hill. Dark blue is a hard color to both target and avoid at nighttime. Suffice it to say that my course took me smack into a big, fat Dutchman and both of us rolled downhill while his musket discharged into thin air. While I lay sprawled, another fat fellow sat down on me, but my immediate desire to throw him off was quelled by the numerous applications of pig-stickers to both sides of my prostrate form. I had been captured and my days as a Confederate infantryman were over. (See Map with X for capture site.)

My disgust at being captured turned quickly into revulsion against my captors for,

I saw but one man in the 136th New York Regiment who could speak English. That was a sergeant by the name of Charles Bedelle who took charge of the prisoners. He told me . . . that two-thirds of them had landed from Germany at Castle Garden, New York, six weeks before. They each received $600 bounty money.[4]

Such were the mercenary forces that were being sent against the South under the twin banners of human liberty and Constitutional Union! By waving their filthy greenbacks over teeming immigration pens of Northern cities, the procurers in Washington showed their true colors—that money rather than love (of liberty or union) was their most effective means of destroying the cause of Southern Independence. Foreigners, who had only recently arrived, seeking respite from the worst of European despotism, were now being herded into the Valley of the Tennessee to deny freedom to a people whose language and history they did not even understand. I'm afraid that the bitterness I felt as a result of these ruminations did not serve me well when I was brought before General Hooker.

I remember General Hooker as a pleasant-looking man who returned my salute like a soldier. As the only non-commissioned officer of the twenty men captured that night, however, it was obvious I had been brought in for interrogation. After asking me about a hundred questions that I stone-walled, Hooker ended our meeting by proclaiming me the "most complete know-nothing for my size he had ever seen."[6] This observation only served to unleash my pent-up bitterness, for I blurted out, "Then sir, I hope you soon see Braxton Bragg for if he had been listening to Old Pete, you and I might have been having this conversation in reverse back in Bridgeport!" Shocked at my own rashness, I never found out if Hooker realized (or cared) what I had just blurted out, for I was immediately ushered out of his presence to join my comrades for the trek into Chattanooga.

Our passage over the Tennessee River was on a pontoon bridge the Yankees had seemingly just thrown up about four miles below Lookout Mountain. Nearing the middle of this bridge, we were halted and formed in two single files on either side to allow a long train of blue-coated officers and staff pass by.

General Grant and General Thomas rode in front (and) when General Grant reached the line of ragged, filthy, bloody, despairing prisoners strung out on each side of the bridge, he lifted his hat and held it over his head until he passed the last man of that living funeral cortege. He was the only officer in that whole train who recognized us and paid military honor to a fallen foe.[7]

Now here I could use the reader's help. When we first reached Chattanooga, some of us noticed that a civilian was taking our picture. This was a distinctly incidental and forgettable thing, considering our dejected circumstances at the time. Years after the war ended, however, I received the picture below in a stack of old newspapers sent to me by a comrade who knew I was compiling relevant materials for my "Rambling Recollections of the Stormy Sixties." Both he and my parents swear that I'm the circled prisoner with the big black hat. The only problem is that yours truly never let his whiskers grow out of control like that circled fellow and I've persisted in denying their claim. To help you decide in my favor, I've provided the accompanying pen-and-ink rendering of a ambrotype taken at Bill Bridges's picture gallery on Pecan Street in Austin, Texas, the day my father, Edward Giles, bought me my famous black hat. I was a young nineteen-year-old enlistee then and a twenty-one-year-old when we were herded into that Yankee holding pen at Chattanooga. If you can see the obvious dissimilarities between the 1861 rendering and the 1863 photograph,

VAL GILES

AUSTIN, TEXAS 1861

CONFEDERATE PRISONERS, CHATTANOOGA 1863

please cast your vote for me by writing to the Texas Commission on the Civil War, Austin, Texas.

To give the devil his due, it seemed that Bragg's plan to starve the Yankees out of Chattanooga was having an effect. Full rations had been reduced to whatever our guards seemed able to improvise or steal. Hollow-cheeked men followed wagons that wasted mules were barely able to pull, fighting over fallen scraps. Some of our guards pulled "trough duty" to keep their comrades from eating the corn fodder allotted to the horses. Off-duty soldiers piled the garbage heaps and a stray dog that wandered near our compound became supper for the night. One ingenious private found a discarded tin can that once served as a candle replete with grease and a rag; he mixed flies in with this grease and wolfed the concoction whole proclaiming, "I ate them all and relished them very much."[8]

After being confined in Chattanooga for two days, we were sent to Bridgeport, Alabama, on November 1, 1863, via a little steamboat called *The Red Rock*. As we were being led into Bridgeport, my anger at Bragg's failure to carry out President Davis's order boiled up anew. Three weeks ago, the First Corps could have seized this now-bustling supply depot before Hooker even arrived, thwarting Grant's plan for relieving Chattanooga. How I yearned to have been a part of Old Pete's alternative rather than winding up a prisoner of Bragg's ineptitude. For succor, I cast an analytic gaze around Bridgeport, forlornly playing the role of some belated scout whose information about Yankee targets and fields of fire could still be of some use to our army and its cause. Alas, from Bridgeport we were loaded on boxcars and shipped north to Nashville where we were interred in the Tennessee

Penitentiary surrounded by convicts and civil prisoners under strong military guard.

The next morning, our party, which had increased to about one hundred and fifty prisoners, was marched up to the depot of the Louisville and Nashville Railroad. On our way to the depot, we passed the residence of Andrew Johnson, who at that time was military governor of Tennessee. Johnson, standing on the gallery of his residence, stopped our column by raising his arm toward the officer of the guard detail. We were then ordered to the sidewalk and formed into two lines facing the old turncoat. Johnson preceded to make a speech allowing that he himself had been born a Southerner and deeply loved his kinsmen, but that we had been led astray in fighting against the best government the world had ever seen. I guess it was speeches like this that caused "the best government" in the world to elect Andrew Johnson its vice president the following year. In seeking to implement a conciliatory reconstruction of the country after Lincoln's death, however, Johnson would become the only president in the history of that government to be impeached. I've often wondered from that day to this if any of his fellow Tennesseans who stood next to me that morning were able to interview the old Judas on the dichotomy between his 1863 speech and the harsh policies of Radical Republicanism, which finally destroyed him. Anyway, Johnson ended his harangue, allowing he would personally pardon any and all of us if we would take the oath of allegiance to the United States. Two who stepped forward to oblige were so hooted and hissed by the unrepentant Johnnies, that the Military Governor of Tennessee waved our gang along, leaving him behind with his two fellow-deserters.

In Louisville, we were confined in an old tobacco

warehouse packed in like herrings in a tin can. Rats as big as Texas fox squirrels scampered around this barn tame as house cats. They galloped all over us at night, attacking our meager provisions in our haversack pillows and even mistaking exposed toes for goobers. Next morning we were shipped over the Ohio River in an old ferry boat named the *John Shallcross,* which put in at Jeffersonville, Indiana. We arrived at Indianapolis about 3 A.M. and were taken to Camp Morton about two miles away. Camp Morton was comprised of about twenty acres and before the war had been the site of the Indiana State Fair Grounds. An old building had been converted into a barracks for rebel prisoners and it was surrounded with a fourteen-foot-high plank fence. On the outside of this fence, a wooden platform about ten-feet high had been built for sentries to walk. There were no signs about leaving hope behind, but many a young rebel would never leave Camp Morton alive.[9]

Upon entering, we were immediately subjected to a petty search and robbed of all personal keepsakes that had no value to a stranger. My loss involved a small diary of daily events that had been placed inside the vest pocket of my jacket. Inside the pages was my only claim to wealth, a lone five-dollar Confederate bill. The greasy little lieutenant who robbed me of my last memento of the South said it was enough to have me shot as a spy in the morning. It did not take me long to realize that we were being guarded by a group of men who had not seen frontline service in the cause of "liberty and Union." Few of these bluecoats had ever loaded a musket in sight of the Stars and Bars or even gotten within earshot of the Rebel Yell.

About one month after our arrival at Camp Morton, news of Bragg's retreat from Missionary Ridge began to circulate the grapevine telegraph, which only added to our feeling of dejection and isolation. It seemed Grant finally had pulled off what everyone except Bragg had predicted. Yankee reinforcements had converged on Chattanooga from Virginia and Mississippi to lift the siege. Now I probably know what the reader of this narrative is thinking at this point: "Here goes Giles again, beating that dead horse about Bragg's failure to carry out the Bridgeport initiative!" Well, I won't this time because the boys in barracks ten conducted a real dispassionate analysis last night as to why Bragg—who blamed every subordinate except Cleburn for the debacle—was his own worst enemy. Here I'll offer a recapitulation of that discussion devoid of my own personal prejudice for a pre-emptive strike against Bridgeport.

Beyond debate, of course, was that Bragg bore sole responsibility for the decision to besiege Chattanooga after our victory at the Brotherton Farm. Not one man present could recall any of his superiors supporting such a tactic. Bragg's assumption that nature had sufficiently strengthened his center via the sheer height of Missionary Ridge furthered his undoing when Grant's attack came on November 25th. It was precisely in the center that the once-disgraced Army of the Cumberland had broken through while the Confederate flanks thwarted Grant's original battle plan, allowing our army to escape via Ringgold.

My contribution to his discussion was to recall a conversation between General Longstreet and his artillery chief, E. Porter Alexander, that I overheard while on guard duty in early October. Colonel Alexander had complained that Bragg's decision to place his artillery on the topographical height of Missionary Ridge would rob it of the effectiveness it would have further down on the military height. Muzzles of guns placed on the topographical height could not be depressed sharply enough to defend Bragg's vaunted "third line" of defense. Subsequent events had apparently proven Alexander correct. One captured artilleryman who had arrived in late November claimed that his battery had been reduced to rolling lit shells down the ridge towards Thomas's unexpected assault.

Longstreet, meanwhile, had criticized Bragg's faith in the first two parallel lines of rifle pits below the topographical crest, comparing them to double stitching on the hem of a garment, i.e., once one ripped, it was only a matter of time before the other one went as well. "Old Pete" then expressed his preference for those enveloping fields of fire that had served us so well at Fredericksburg and later at Pipe Creek, Maryland, in July. Apparently the only good such opposition to Bragg served was to cause him to detach the First Corps from his impending, self-induced defeat and send it up to Knoxville two weeks before Grant attacked. We must have analyzed the defeat at Chattanooga most of the night, for it seemed my head barely hit my haversack when we were summoned for morning mail call and the drawing of our daily ration. I had no way of knowing then that events growing from these simple routines would create in me an intense desire to escape to the South.

One of the bluecoat shirkers I referred to above was Corporal Pheiffer, who dispensed the prisoners' mail after each letter had been opened and examined at headquarters. It was his wont to mount a soapbox every morning in front of the sutler's store, call out the names of recipients and quiz each as to from whom a letter was expected. Upon receiving the proper response, he would make the most vile comments about the sender and toss the letter over the heads of the crowd. The morning after our post-Chattanooga "round table," Pheiffer started by calling the name of a young Kentuckian taken in that assault by asking from whom he expected a letter. "From my sister in Louisville," the young prisoner eagerly responded, not knowing of the corporal's despicable routine. With a profane remark, which I cannot repeat here, accompanied by a smirk at his own dirty joke, Pheiffer flung the letter high in the air. Before that letter began its descent, however, our little Yankee mailman had himself been hurled a good six-feet backward off his soapbox, landing with a thud against the sutler's wall. He had received a fine lesson in manners from one rebel who still possessed enough strength and self-respect to rise above the collective despair of Camp Morton in that winter of 1863. Of course, the new prisoner was immediately hurried off to the guardhouse despite a rising storm of protest coming from the throats of his fellow detainees.

Without any doubt, we knew there were cruel men who staffed the prisoner-of-war camps on both sides of the Mason-Dixon Line. Indeed, the only man executed for war crimes during America's most costly conflict was William Wirz, the commandment of Andersonville Prison (although a Southern victory might have found a Wirz or two living north of the Potomac!). Nevertheless, despite geography or politics, there will always be those behind the firing lines who prefer administering punishment against those taken captive in battle, i.e., "An ambitious coward loves authority where he is secure from danger and can vent his fiendish nature on his fellow man." It seemed to me from what happened next, however, that the incompetent administrators of Camp Morton were careless to the precipitation of a riot, which could have caused a loss of life to prisoners and guards alike.

As the unruly Confederates moved off to receive their rations, some still booing and hissing the treatment of the young Kentuckian, a blue-belly sergeant at the supply wagon called out that the daily ration was being reduced to eight ounces of bread and one-quarter pound of "blue beef" in retaliation for the starvation being visited on Federal prisoners at Andersonville and Libby Prisons. This announcement proved to be the quick match that lit the fuse shortened by that morning's mail-call incident.

Almost as one—I among them—the prisoners surged forward from their double lines, dispatching the guards around the commissary wagon and, in a desperate grab for food, literally tearing this conveyance apart. Shots rang out above the melee and I was aware of several on the perimeter of our unruly mob who fell, which only served to incite those at the center to even greater exertions. Some of the more daring (or desperate) began to shout, "To the arsenal. Get the muskets!" Surprisingly, these shouts actually seemed to give the crowd pause since most knew (or should have known) that the arsenal was a considerable distance outside the fence and part of the officer's billet. Through all this confusion, I noted old Colonel Stephens, the camp commandant, rushing as fast as his fat legs could carry him toward the small infirmary located in the far northeast corner of our enclosure. I was tempted to dismiss this withdrawal as the natural act of the coward who was responsible for all our misery, but Stephens quickly emerged, escorting a young Yankee officer toward the milling prisoners. As he reached the halfway mark, the colonel wildly motioned a sergeant back to the guardhouse from whence he had just emerged on the run leading an armed squad toward us. It was at this point that I noticed the young officer accompanying the commandant had but one leg, his speedy yet obviously painful course being aided by a crude crutch and the frenetic urgings of Colonel Stephens. What happened next probably served to quell the largest uprising in Indiana's history but, as I indicated above, gave me my greatest impetus to escape.

Approaching the platform, which stood in front of the now-destroyed wagon, Colonel Stephens probably saved his life by literally wrapping a tattered Confederate battle flag around his shoulders as he paused to assist his young companion up the steps. Even at that, he received several good blows from his unruly guests. Waving the tattered banner silently above them both, Stephens turned the crowd's jeers to cheers by suddenly pointing toward the guardhouse where the recently-interred Kentuckian could be seen walking freely toward us. "Men," the colonel intoned, "I have reviewed the facts involving this morning's mail-call and have determined that Corporal Pheiffer breached proper procedure in the execution of his duties. He has been reduced in rank and the prisoner is released to you with my compliments. I will leave the matter of your rations to Lieutenant Gabriel. Sir, the platform is yours."[10]

All eyes became fixed on this new figure in our prison. He was about six-foot, fair of complexion with somber blue eyes and a shock of blond hair cascading from the back of a somewhat dusty campaign hat. He stood using his crutch more like a staff, placed a half-arm's length in front of him rather than tucked under his armpit as most invalids would. Gabriel addressed us thusly and I remember many of his words as if they were spoken yesterday.

Soldiers of the South. Regarding your food ration, I have only the last paragraph of my last letter to my father written the day I gained the heights of Missionary Ridge to sustain you. With your permission, I would like to share it with you in hope that it provides you with the nourishment it gives to me in overcoming depleted resources. (A pause, a look from Gabriel and silent assent from the crowd.) The first dead rebel I had ever seen, Father was not over fifteen years of age and very slender in size. He was clothed in a cotton suit, and was barefooted; barefooted in that cold, wet November. I examined his haversack. For a day's ration there was a handful of black beans, a few pieces of sorghum and a half-dozen roasted acorns. That was an infinitely poor outfit for marching and fighting, but that Tennessee Confederate had made it answer his purpose.[11]

The young lieutenant folded the letter and looked up and over the crowd of prisoners, which had now grown as quiet as church mice. Colonel Stephens, meanwhile, was casting nervous glances from Gabriel and back toward the crowd as if determining whether to make another dash to the rear while the good order lasted. He seemed to be startled, however, by what Gabriel did next. Taking the tattered battle flag from the old colonel's shoulders, Gabriel held it before us and closed with these words:

My leg was left at Ringgold, Georgia, but I would like to offer you the standard found near that young soldier's body. According to the regulations regarding prisoners, you can not display it in this camp, but I will offer pieces of it to those who wish to honor his sacrifice by drawing rations that he could never hope for. For those who favor nursing their own discomfort, do not take a part of this standard nor show up for today's ration, for none will be issued to those without this badge of sacrifice. Colonel, if you will do the honors, I will return to the infirmary.

Well, just about all of us fell in to get the most-prized ration ticket ever issued during the War Between the States. We displayed our tattered shares of the banner at every mess call with that strange mix of pride and humility that we had felt after Gabriel finished addressing us. I have it with me still, for it went with me the night I escaped—November 8, 1864, the second victory of Abraham Lincoln. As for Gabriel, I never saw him again after watching him hobble back to the Camp Morton infirmary to complete his treatment. Most of the reason for that, of course, was due to my renewed desire to rejoin my comrades-in-arms, one of whom had been the young Tennessean sacrificed on the altar of Bragg's ineptitude.

When I first made my determination to escape, no one, including yours truly, could have guessed that my best opportunity would be occasioned by an illness, which dispatched me to a pest hole outside of camp. Smallpox made its appearance in October 1864 nearly a year after my capture at Wauhatchie. On November 1st, the camp surgeon informed me that I had a "beautiful case of varioloid" and ordered me to the pest hospital about two miles from the main compound where I could "die comfortably." The conditions I found in this barnlike structure were loathsome, partly because the patients seemed to be suffering from a more advanced stage of this disease than I. The young fellow in the cot next to mine went by the name of Jack Warefield and I knew him only as one of those daredevils who had made several desperate escape attempts back at Camp Morton. Although I had been asked to join in one of these, I had refused under the conviction that actual success varied inversely with the numbers making the attempt, i.e., the fewer the merrier, so to speak.

Jack had made a study of the flooring in that old barn

and, whether by accident or design, he had "found" a loose plank right under his cot. There normally were four guards on the outside and one on the inside of our pesthouse, but the soldier who came in for duty around mid-night on November 8, 1864 was dead drunk and had fallen asleep in a chair by the stove. I reckon he and his immediate superior were all good Republicans who could be forgiven for an overly-rambunctious celebration of Abe's second Presidential victory. At any rate, Abe's good fortune turned out to be contagious for two suffering rebels that night as Jack leaned over and whispered, "Now is the time!"

We eased ourselves down through the hole under Jack's cot and crawled out to the edge of the building where the lattice-work had fallen down, peering out at a steady snowfall all the time. It was mighty cold for two patients in prison rags, but I felt most of my shivering was due to excited anticipation of escape rather than the temperature. As best as we could determine, the two guards meeting to our front were the ones patrolling the north and east side of the pesthouse. The two we couldn't see must have been over to the south and west sides of the building, so we decided not to worry about them. The two meeting to our front were heavily-bundled against the storm with cloaks and heavy gloves. They halted briefly in front of our hiding place (I thought they'd hear my heart pounding!) and, after a muffled greeting, moved off in opposite directions. When they got about twenty yards apart, Jack touched my shoulder and we began our sprint. We were urged on to even greater efforts by the duet of the guards calling, "Halt! Halt! Turn out the guard." These guards were so bundled up, however, that we had covered more than a hundred yards before they were able to fire. Their missives went wide and the snow began to cover our tracks in silent sheets.

We skirted Indianapolis and struck a turnpike running parallel to the White River about two miles below the city—we were now heading south. As I glanced toward my companion, I realized the worst of our ordeal still lay ahead of us. We were marked indelibly as escaped Southern prisoners from out tattered garb and lice-infested hair to our varioloid-pitted countenances and Southern accents. We knew also that a small detachment of cavalry was kept at Camp Morton for the express purpose of recapturing escaped prisoners and that as the storm abated, such scouts could easily pick up our tracks in the new-fallen snow. A lot of luck would have to marry-up with personal cunning if Jack and I were to get south of the Ohio River. Even then, our escape was not guaranteed in the border states of 1864.

Meanwhile, our first natural obstacle was a frozen tributary of the White River, for the ice was obviously too thin to hold our weight. Below the ford, Jack spied an old foot log that was covered with ice and slick as glass. Jack suggested we "coon" it by clambering across on all fours. It was after we had successfully completed this venture that I realized my hands were in danger of freezing. Both of us were now pretty fagged out as the gray dawn appeared. Almost simultaneously, we both spied a huge snow-mound about two hundred yards off the road in an open field. We guessed it to be a large haymow that might offer some shelter but, being in an open field, our tracks could easily give our position away. As I said earlier, Jack was a real daredevil who seemingly had a plan for every contingency. "Let's climb the fence and walk backwards," he said, "that'll fool 'em." So that was the method we used to reach our first shelter after escaping. We went backwards at the oblique for about two hundred yards and, sure enough, found a great stack of a hay rick with a huge hole eaten out of the south side by the nearby cattle. We crawled in and covered the entrance with straw, falling quickly into an exhausted sleep.

When we emerged from our shelter around nightfall, we were heartened to see that a new snowfall had obliterated our tracks, but the pangs of hunger now assailing us would not disappear so easily. Only a few rotten apples had kept us from collapsing during our hazardous journey thus far. Strangely, our failure to exit the road before sunrise this day occasioned our first full meal since escaping Camp Morton. Rounding a bend in the road, Jack and I were espied by a woman who had suddenly emerged from a nearby cabin with a pail of slops. Throwing caution to the wind, Jack, who had a lone counterfeit greenback on his person, whispered, "We'll tackle that lady for breakfast," as he ushered me boldly into the front yard. "Madam, can you furnish us with breakfast this morning?" my daredevil companion asked, bowing politely and doffing his cap. "We are hungry and will gladly pay you."

The woman, eyeing us both for a while, knocked the ashes from her corncob pipe and replied cautiously, "I guess so if you can eat sich as we've got." Well, Jack's daring paid off handsomely in a meal of fresh pork, cornbread, pumpkin and sweet potatoes. The woman and Jack did all the talking and her questions about our appearance in that neck of the woods were getting pretty warm, but Jack, being one of the smoothest prevaricators I had ever met, was equal to the task. Upon presenting the counterfeit greenback, he even wheedled a substantial lunch from the woman when she confessed her lack of sufficient change. Nonetheless, the minute we passed from sight of her cabin, I let Jack know how I felt about cheating our benefactress. "Oh, don't let a little thing like that worry your conscience," he said, "Under ordinary circumstances it would be a mean trick, but necessity knows no law. All is fair in war."

Later that day, having secured shelter and a good nap in a dried-out creek bed, Jack and I built a small fire to cook our lunch and discuss our future plans. It turned out we agreed on nothing. Jack was determined to play the Yankee bounty system for all it was worth. Indiana, like most Northern states at this time, was finding itself with more money than patriots in holding the Union together. Men of means were paying $1,000 to $5,000 for substitutes to go to the front. The poor in each community had a choice of being shot at as poor men or shot at while sporting a handsome bounty in their pockets. It was Jack's idea to go into some town and hire out as substitutes to two men of means, then complete our travels as gentlemen. I found this suggestion abominable.

> I was hiding out and dodging through the country as an escaped prisoner of war and I was not going to add disgrace to my unpleasant position by deserting the Confederacy and joining the Yankee army. That was a little more than I could stand and I told Jack emphatically that I would not go with him.[12]

After lunch, we divided our remaining rations, shook hands over the now-dying fire, and Jack took his leave. Although he was a daredevil, with uncommon good looks and obviously well-educated, there was something unfathomable about my fellow refugee, whom I was never to see again. Jack Warefield's story about his past was believable as far as it went, but I always had the feeling something important had been left out in the telling.

Nonetheless, a feeling of loneliness and dejection swept over me when I realized his departure has left me all alone, an ailing fugitive without resources in enemy territory.

I was now sick at heart as well as in body for the varioloid had spread all over me, swelling my face, feet and hands. Despite the extinguished fire, I began to sweat profusely, reaching almost unconsciously into empty pockets for some handkerchief with which to mop my brow. My right hand came back, clutching a tattered piece of cloth almost unrecognizable in my stupefied state, now being further assailed by the icy blasts of an approaching Indiana blizzard. As I touched the cloth to my face, however, it enlivened other sensations. It was comfortably warm and contained the faint, familiar odor of gunpowder co-mingled with pine smoke. Simultaneously, both recognition and resolution brought me to my feet with a quickness I thought long gone, for the cloth was none other than the remnant of Lieutenant Gabriel's Confederate banner brought down from the heights of Missionary Ridge. Tucking my share of the ripped standard into my breast pocket, I scrambled up to the road and turned my steps southward, away from the approaching storm.

I had not gone more than two miles before I was suddenly overtaken by a sleigh coming from behind at a two-forty gait as if the driver was determined to outrace the storm. There was no time for me to get off the road and the driver, probably more startled than curious, pulled up sharply on the harness of his fine-looking black horse and called out, "Hello—what's the matter with you?"

"Got a light case of chicken pox," I replied.

"Chicken pox! You've got the smallpox and are in a pretty bad row of stumps."

Needless to say, the man's pinpoint diagnosis of my condition and his persistence were making me mighty nervous, so I tried to push him along his way by some caustic remark about him being a physician. This stratagem backfired, for the stranger replied,

> As a matter of fact, I am a physician. Dr. Evans C. Dyal at your service. I have an old vacant house down in my field about a mile from here and I suggest you allow me to quarantine you there, for if I leave you on th is road in this condition, you will certainly die.[13]

Resigned, I entered the sleigh, was thankfully offered part of the doctor's lap robe, and we were off, with my fevered mind not really grasping what turned out to be an uncommon turn of good fortune. We entered his field through a back gate and approached an old log cabin that stood below the swale of a hill upon which I noticed the main residence. In an age that had adopted the convenience of easily-applied labels—i.e., Unionist, Secesh, Republican and Copperhead—Dr. Dyal had referred to himself during our ride as a "War Democrat," liberal in his social views but a staunch Unionist. Giving me the lap robe, he bade me enter the cabin, promising to send me bedding, medicine, and victuals in short order. I never imagined that I would spend three weeks in that old cabin under "the watchful eye of that true friend of suffering humanity."

Dr. Dyal was seldom home during the day since spotted fever was then raging all over the country. He was a devoted physician and a well-read student of those current issues dividing his neighborhood and country. His hired boy, Jake, was commissioned to keep me supplied with my immediate wants as well as some of the leading newspapers, which I read thoroughly. Jake was not any company, however, for he would leave these items at the door, knock once and be gone over the hill like a frightened turkey. After about a week of this routine, I was left a copy of the *Indianapolis Journal* and the following AD jumped out at me from the front page:

REWARD

The government will pay $30.00 each for the capture and return to Camp Morton the following-described escaped prisoners of war: One JACKSON W. WAREFIELD (regiment unknown) about five feet, eight inches high, dark complexion hair and moustache very black, weighs one hundred and fifty pounds, age twenty-six; One VAL GILES, Company B, Fourth Texas Regiment, Rebel army, six feet high, hair dark and long, eyes brown, weighs one hundred and forty pounds, age nineteen years.

A. A. Stephens,
Colonel Commanding Camp Morton
W. P. Davidson, Adjutant

I was well aware from previous discussions with my host that companies of the home-guard had been organized all over southern Indiana for the purpose of arresting Copperheads, catching deserters from the Federal Army, and rounding up escaped Confederate prisoners. The only solace I had after consigning the reward notice to the flames, was that it had mistakenly given my age at enlistment three years ago. The next morning, when Dr. Dyal stopped by before making his rounds, I told him I felt fine enough to light out that morning. He looked at me for a while and motioned me to a stool before addressing me thusly:

George, you are one of the smoothest and most cheerful prevaricators I have ever met, and I'll tell you why I say so. I graduated in medicine in Philadelphia in 1855 and two of my most intimate friends at college were Southern men, one from Georgia and one from Louisiana. I roomed with the young fellow from Georgia for more than two years and became familiar with Southern manners their accent on words and I came to know a Southern accent whenever I hear a man speak. You are not a native of Ohio as you say you are or any other state north of the Ohio River. You "reckon so" while a northern man would say I "guess so."[14]

Well, I "reckon" the good doctor could tell his words were making me nervous, for he quickly assured me that he was my friend and that I could trust him. After hearing his assurances and aware of his past ministrations to me, my whole story came out in one flood. It was a great relief to tell the truth to someone who could be trusted after living a lie so long and I slept better that night than any since my capture. Several days later, Jake brought me a new suit of clothes and after a bath and shave, I was invited to Dr. Dyal's main residence as a seal of our compact, which included a new, mutually-agreed-to alibi that would sit well with the home-guard. Little did I know how soon we would have to use it.

Three nights later as I was setting into the feather mattress of the guest room, I was startled by the sounds of multiple hoof-beats galloping into the front yard. After listening to my host greet the riders who were obviously too numerous to be patients, Dr. Dyal appeared in my doorway to announce, "Captain James of the home-guard wants to see you. Light out old boy and I will tell him you are quartered down at the cabin hoping to lead him hence." When I heard the men gallop away toward my former refuge, I let myself out the back window, which opened onto a low-lying porch roof. I was soon splitting moonbeams in the opposite direction of the home-guard—due south once again. I never saw the good doctor again although I wrote to him after returning to Texas in September 1865. He wrote back explaining how, in accompanying the guard to my cabin and thence to a neighbor's house represented to them as my friend, he had been unable to slip the fee earned from his last patient into my new suit. I am satisfied that he told me the truth and we have communicated several times since then.

Ironically, the final leg of my escape from the sovereign state of Indiana was expedited by an intelligence I had gained from the woman who had provided Jack and me with our first meal after escaping Camp Morton. She had told us that her husband was away seeking his fortune in the saw-log industry then sweeping through the southern part of the state. Thousands of big trees were being cut and floated down White River and the Wabash to the Ohio where they were constructed into rafts for transit down to Grant's old headquarters at Cairo, Illinois. The husband of our hostess had apparently traveled fifty-miles south to Pigeon Creek and I determined to explain my solitary sojourn southward in like manner. My alibi was considerably strengthened by an axe I had liberated from a deserted woodpile near the road. As Jack had said back at that old woman's cabin, "All's fair in war."

Continuing along in the guise of my new vocation, I noted that mine was not the only act of vandalism in that neighborhood. The once heavily-forested hills of southern Indiana were then being ravished in a manner that was wholesale exploitation of nature's bounty no matter who won the war. Unlike the saw-log industry to which I was ascribing my destination, the tan-bark industry was destroying beautiful red oaks, which were left to rot after being stripped of their bark, while the kiln-waste was dumped into the White River. Although men were being paid handsomely for this work, I would have none of it, for the sights and smells of the neighborhood sickened me. It seemed that in order to preserve the Union, the Yankees had unleashed a powerful machine that was destroying what was most attractive in the American landscape. The perception that this machine was creeping slowly southward in support of the foreign mercenaries who had captured me, served to quicken my steps toward Dixie.

It proved impossible to get below the Ohio River, however, without supporting my alibi with some axe work. Numerous bands of lumbermen began soliciting my labor with ever-increasing frequency from shacks, cooking fires and work sites within easy view of others in the vicinity whose job-offers I had just spurned. I realized one could only turn down so many jobs without drawing scowls or worst yet, suspicion as to my motives. The promise of a thirty-dollar reward and a government-sponsored trip to Indianapolis would be fine fare for these patriotic Hoosiers who had stayed behind to despoil the landscape in order to defeat the "planter aristocracy" of the South. I had several close calls after leaving Dr. Dyal, but none closer than those that relied on a fiddle and a handshake.

About a week after leaving the doctor's house, I was literally pulled into a workcrew crossing the road toward their cabin after a day in the woodlot on the opposite side. There were five of these lumbermen in such a hearty, raucous mood that any refusal on my part to join them as the sun began to set would have seemed odd indeed. These fellows worked for an absentee landlord who provided the cabin, victuals and twenty dollars per month for sixteen-hour days of woodcutting. When I meekly protested that I was not deserving of sharing their hearty supper, the largest of the crew said, "George, you can earn your share by filling up Cookie's wood-box yonder. There's some logs right outside." Well, I chopped for about one-half hour with my axe, which proved not to be the sharpest one in Indiana. "Cookie" looked out before long and asked if I was near ready since the "boys" were getting famished. As I appeared in the doorway with my armload of wood, the crew turned from their observation of one of their number seated in a corner and immediately the whole place went dead silent. My right hand was bleeding profusely from its unaccustomed labor. "Pretty tender hand for a woodsman, George," quipped their spokesman. "What crew were you workin' for up north?" At that moment, the seated man in the corner stood up to place an old fiddle on a crude shelf and, in so doing, probably saved my bacon.

"To tell the truth, boys, I've been doing all my sawing with that implement Red just laid down," I replied, nodding toward their previous object of interest. "That's how I've been earning my keep through these camps." The faces of my once-suspicious hosts brightened as if on cue. "You mean you can play that thing?" the frustrated musician with the red beard asked, jerking his huge thumb back toward the fiddle. Answering in the affirmative, it immediately became evident from the collective reaction that I had assured my popularity amongst these denizens of the wood. After a hearty supper of pork, bacon, beans, molasses and cornbread, I offered up a silent prayer of thanks to my maternal grandmother who had given me fiddle lessons as a boy back in Austin. I then proceeded to "saw" away at the few hoe-downs I knew, including "Hog Eye," "Billy in the Low Ground," and "Polly, Put the Kettle On," as "those brawny, rail-splitting log-rollers pranced, capered and shuffled all over the room." They kept this racket up until eleven o'clock when I positively refused to saw any longer. Despite the next day being Sunday, those fellows were up before daylight promising me permanent room and board if I would only stay on as their fiddler. Upon my positing my need to rendezvous with a relative further south, they wished me well, gave me a lunch, and I went on my way refreshed and not a little relieved since from what my companions had said, I was nearing the Ohio River.

Since my departing Camp Morton, the buildings set nearest my escape route were neither primary residences nor the rustic camps of loggers, but rather those small, white clapboard churches of the Methodist denomination. Normally, such buildings were deserted and could be passed without any thought given to evasive action on the fugitive's part. Emboldened by this fact, I more than once sought a late-night refuge in the solid woodsheds of these sanctuaries. In forgetting that today was Sunday, however, I found myself completely unprepared for the encounter which next threatened to unmask my identity.

A small throng of people had apparently just emerged from worship in one of these structures set about twenty-five feet from the road on which I was now walking. They seemed to be swaying back and forth in a highly-agitated manner that I mistook for some post-service ritual. Just as I directed my steps to the far side of the road, however, first one and then a second young man broke from the crowd and made a beeline for yours truly. Instinctively, I switched my axe to my left hand in order to present a less hostile demeanor toward these men and to lessen the chance that they might seek to grab the implement. Just as the first youth (about my age) crashed into my now-free right arm, I realized he was being pursued by the second man who matched my six-feet, but who was more muscular in girth (not a great feat since I had just escaped from a year's captivity thanks to smallpox!). Holding the first fellow at arm's length by his Sunday finery, I halted the second by holding up my axe-head butt first so it wouldn't appear I was out to murder him on the spot. "C'mon, lads," I said as calmly as I could muster, "there shouldn't be any fighting on the Sabbath. Let it wait a day." By this time the three of us were completely surrounded by the congregation whose members were shouting for their favorite champion. I didn't know how much longer I could keep the larger one at bay with my hammerhead as he was circling me and the smaller lad who seemed only too happy that I was keeping between him and his pursuer. Thankfully for that moment at least, the parson emerged from the church and called the flock into the yard with many an earnest entreaty including the observation that the commotion was causing some of the spooked carriage horses to pull loose from the hitching post.

As the minister approached the three of us still out in the road, my heart skipped a few beats. This man, who had a long white mane framing a handsomely-lined face, was familiar to me in the only way he could be at this place and time in my life. He was one of two Methodist ministers who had ridden the circuit up to my former prison camp, a staunch Unionist who blended his belief about loyalty to the Union with sermons about divine redemption. More telling was the fact that I had helped him unload bandages and blankets brought up to the pesthouse on at least two occasions after being consigned there. I knew him as Reverend Gordon and there was no time to run from my now-precarious predicament. I had

heard enough from the crowd to know they had been actuated by some bitter political issue of the war and many of
them were still milling about in the churchyard. My only
hope of avoiding detection now lay in my relatively new
suit of clothes and the fact that my once-pasty, pock-
marked face was now ruddy and weather-beaten from the
elements.

"Blessed be the Peacemakers," Gordon intoned with
a warm smile, extending his hand toward the one I had
just released from the younger man's collar. "John," he
said, addressing this smaller combatant, "what is the
meaning of this outrage?" Well, "John" turned out to be
the parson's son and the tale he told was not an unusual
one for southern Indiana during "the Stormy Sixties." It
appears that a young lady had snatched a butternut
breast-pin from the larger man, which was the Copperhead emblem, and stomped it under her foot. The Southern sympathizer reacted by saying he wouldn't hit a
woman, but would gladly thrash any man who cheered
her action. It seems young John Gordon was fleeing the
fact that he was about to become the third Unionist to hit
the dirt of the churchyard when I happened along. Now
things started warming up for yours truly. After admon-
ishing his son to shake my hand as well as that of the copperhead who had returned to the churchyard in search of
his pin, Reverend Gordon turned his full attention to me.

"You seem mighty familiar to me, Mister, Mister . . . "
("Walker,") I volunteered.)

"Have we met during one of my swings up north? I've
preached at Bloomington and Martinsville."

Since he specified two places I had never been, the
preacher kept me from lying twice on the Sabbath.

"Not likely, sir," I replied. "I was christened a Baptist
and have never visited those two towns."

"Well, no mind," he rejoined, "you must join my family and me for dinner up at the Manse. It's your first driveway on the right after leaving here and John and I will be up there directly after closing the church and collecting the womenfolk. I'm sure they would like to thank you for bringing a bit of pacificity to our neck of the woods. Go up there and let yourself in. We'll be along directly."

I felt trapped by the minister's firm invitation. It seemed every muscle in my throat had been strained in an effort to mask my Texas drawl during our short exchange. There was no way I could continue the masquerade in front of an entire family whose sire seemed convinced he had met me on one of his trips to the northern part of the state.

Unwittingly, the minister's sudden admonition to the departing copperhead gave me a slim chance of escape. "Tom," Reverend Gordon called, "you are still welcome in our fold. Please join John and me in expressing thanks to Mr. Walker for his peace-keeping effort." Tom, the copperhead, turned slowly back toward us and his former mood seemed abated by the fact he had retrieved his butternut pin, which he was now inserting back into his lapel. Suddenly I recalled that while in prison, I had attended two or three clandestine meetings of the Knights of the Golden Circle, a Southern organization that also existed throughout several of the border states. Many copperheads in southern Indiana belonged to the K.G.C.s, yet all I had learned was the handgrip and signal of distress. As the ruffian grudgingly extended his hand at the admonition of his minister, I nervously gave him the grip as best as I remembered it. Startled, he went ramrod stiff on me.

"That's all right, Mr. Walker," he said, a wry smile crossing his lips. "Both the pastor and I are beholdin' to you. Perhaps our paths will cross again," and with that, he trudged off down the pike leaving me alone with my unwanted dinner host. Turning toward his church, the reverend proposed a bet I sincerely hoped he would lose. "Get along to the house now, Mr. Walker. I'll bet we catch up to you in the dray before you reach our driveway.

Like a prisoner headed for the dock, I moved off in the direction indicated. Sure enough, before I got two hundred yards down the road, I heard the sound of a horse and carriage coming behind me. Suddenly, a hushed command emanated from a large oak on the left of the road—"Walk this way, Walker, nice and slow-like." Turning back toward the approaching vehicle as if to let it come up on my right, I gave a half-hearted wave to its occupants and stooped as if to lay my axe down in the grass on the left of the highway. Carefully depositing my faithful implement, I dove headfirst toward the oak behind which Tom sat on a sorrel mare at the head of what looked like a mighty slippery bridal path running down through the woods. "Get on," he ordered and off we sped, me clinging on for dear life as we slid down the muddy defile into a shallow stream-bed running at right angles to the road above. If the good minister or his family let out any sound of surprise at my hasty departure, it never reached my ears.

It seemed we splashed through that stream-bed the remainder of the afternoon before Tom Copperhead (he never divulged his last name) turned south as darkness fell. We dismounted once to consume some cornbread and hog jowl, a "more meager fare," my companion joked than I might have enjoyed with Reverend Gordon's family. My benefactor informed me that he could take me to a boat-landing called Taylorsville on the Indiana side of the Ohio River and advance me passage over to Kentucky. If I could get up to Owensville ten or twelve miles distant, I would find a Major Walker Taylor who was in that part of the state gathering recruits for the Confederate army. The major, Tom explained, had his force scattered along the south bank of the Ohio, waiting for orders to join Lee by spring. It seemed as if my long sojourn to return the Army of Northern Virginia was slowly coming to an end.

The Ohio was running pretty strong the night I crossed over to Kentucky and the oarsmen, who had extracted a handsome fee from Tom Copperhead, did nothing but complain about the unusual warm snap that had swollen the river with melted snow. Thanks to his constant complaining and the strength of the current, we landed about a mile below our starting point where I was unceremoniously deposited without so much as a fare-thee-well. Nonetheless, I was thankful to be across and, without stopping to rest, made my way up to Owensboro arriving just before daybreak.

At Owensboro I soon located Major Walker Taylor who had been commissioned to gather recruits for the Confederate army. He had enlisted about one hundred men, mostly young Kentuckians, who were scattered out among the hills, five and six in a bunch, waiting for orders to go south—"an order that never came." I joined the command with several other escaped prisoners with the understanding we would make our way to Lee's army in early spring.

When I reported to Major Taylor, I looked every bit the tramp. The suit Dr. Dyal had provided me was now soaked, grimy, and ripped from the ordeal of my last sprint from Yankeedom. Upon learning that I had been a "frontliner" in the Army of Northern Virginia for two years, however, my new companions brought forth a tub and a fine suit of gray, compliments of the Ladies Sewing

Circle of Webster, Kentucky. (They are thought of fondly to this day!) In addition, when we left the next morning to check on the Major's strung-out command, yours truly was mounted on a fine gray horse named "Peagram" that had been "liberated" from an old Unionist who had fallen into a bad habit of piloting Yankee cavalry through the neighborhood.

Woe to old Kentucky and to those who wore and rode the gray in the closing months of the war. Throughout all the outrages, horrors, and fiendish deeds being perpetuated in the "dark land," it seemed our major business was running. We were chased by Federal cavalry, ambushed by home guards, and spied on by Unionist civilians. "I saw more retreating while I was with Major Taylor than all Lee's army had done during the entire war."[15]

There was soon to appear in my life, however, a silver lining amongst the dark clouds that were now gathering over the Southland and the cause for which I had struggled to play a part. Her name was Annie and through her came a reconciliation between my personal history and the cause of Southern Independence. It is to her that my final chapter of "Ramblin' Recollections" will be eternally dedicated. All this happened in the following way.[16]

"Texas," said Captain Mannie Taylor as we rode down the Brandenburg Pike at the head of his company early in the spring of 1865,

I am going to spend the night with an old aristocrat . . . and I want you to go with me. He and my father were at college together and were great cronies. He has two splashing girls just as pretty as pinks and bully good Rebs. I've known them always (but) now that they have grown to be young ladies, they call me 'Captain.'[17]

Having been absent some time from both the haunts of aristocrats and the company of ladies, I freely consented to this invitation. Captain Mannie Taylor was the nephew of our commanding officer (although I never gave up hope of rejoining my old command), about two years older than I and, as it turned out, my last close comrade-in-arms during the "Stormy Sixties." We soon concocted what seemed at the time to be a necessary ploy for introducing me into high society. The rank of second sergeant in Hood's old Texas Brigade was impressive enough for the young Kentuckians cavorting along behind us, but Captain Mannie convinced me that a much higher rank was needed to swing wide the door of welcome at "the Colonel's" mansion.

To this end, my companion produced two gold stars from his vest pocket, which he represented as a too-belated gift for honoring his uncle's last promotion. "To our hosts," he said handing me the stars, "you will be Major Giles on his way to rejoin Lee's Army of Northern Virginia!" Since only half of this identity was fabricated, I gleefully pinned on the proffered badges of high society. After Captain Taylor gave some instructions to his first lieutenant about that night's bivouac, we left the command at a gallop along a shaded bridal path that appeared off to our right.

We were soon in sight of the mansion, which stood on a picturesque hillside, about five-hundred yards from the Ohio River. It was a fine two-story, red-brick building, with a gallery in front that ran the length of the house, supported by modest white columns. As we dismounted, I inexplicably felt the coarse layers of experience that had enveloped my spirit since Wauhatchie begin slowly to peel away.

A young Irish servant girl met us at the door, took

our hats and ushered us into the parlor, informing us with her funny English that Colonel R—— would be down in a few minutes. An air of elegance that I had never experienced surrounded me and I made some offhand remark to Captain Taylor as we seated ourselves that life in such a rural retreat would be more enjoyable than chasing about the countryside bushwacking and being bushwacked. Before he could reply, the Colonel appeared in the doorway with one of his daughters on his arm. After the rigors of army life, imprisonment, and escape, the Colonel appeared to be the healthiest, most-robust, well-fed civilian I had seen since leaving Texas. As his daughter curtsied gracefully, the Colonel rushed forward to warmly embrace Captain Taylor, pumping him with numerous questions about his father, whom our host obviously held in high regard. Captain Mannie, however, seeking cover from this barrage, turned toward me, gestured grandly and proclaimed, "Allow me to present Major Giles of the Virginia Army." After bowing to the Colonel as best I could and double-dipping at the introduction of his daughter, Clara, it became my turn to serve as the object of our host's interrogatories. After answering a few easy ones about the engagements I had been in, the old man hit me with clincher, i.e, "Aren't you rather young to hold such a high rank, Major Giles?"

"Oh, no," I replied, starting to sweat, "there are many officers in the Confederate army younger than me"—quickly rattling off the names of young Pelham, Wade, and the Colonel of the Eleventh Mississippi. Undeterred, the Colonel adamantly leaned forward as if to hit me with a follow-up about my age when I was rescued by the appearance in our midst of the most beautiful creature ever beheld by these twenty-three-year-old eyes.

"Major Giles," piped up Taylor as we bounded to our feet. "Allow me to present Miss Annie."

I think it was Plato who once said that the ideal could only be perceived by the mind and not the senses. If this allegation was true, it's for sure the old boy had never stood in a new major's boots as Miss Annie, hair and eyes as black as a Tennessee raven, glided toward him with alabaster hand extended and a smiling, "Pleasure to meet you, Major Plato," sounding through his reddening ears like music from an aeolian harp. That's about as sensual as this scribbler can get to prove a point—that Miss Annie appeared to me as the ideal of Southern beauty even as her independence was being threatened by inept defenders and the approaching tramp of mercenary arms.

Up until this point, my "Ramblin' Recollection of the Stormy Sixties" has flowed pretty easy. I wrote freely about my experiences during this time and hopefully how I felt about those experiences, but I was about to learn that the old Greek philosopher was right about one thing. I am now convinced that the depth of those tender feelings that developed between Miss Annie and myself during that Kentucky spring of 1865 lie far beyond the talents of any writer or orator to put into words. "Heard melodies are sweet, but those unheard are sweeter," observed that philosopher's successors and that's where I'll leave it. Suffice it to say, as I intimated above, that it was through my newfound love that I discovered a reconciliation between my personal trials and the final chapter of the War Between the States.

Our sanctuary, from which the above transformation took place, was a rocky promontory overlooking the Ohio River aptly called "Lover's Leap." Whenever I reached there before my companion, I experienced strange feelings, which she would later describe with a French term, "déjà vu." The name of our hideaway had its origins, Miss Annie explained, in the folklore of savages who had inhabited this land long before Daniel Boone. The capital of this Indian nation had stood near the site of present-day Brandenburg and it was home to the Chief and his only daughter who was "very beautiful," according to my narrator. (I reckon all squaws are beautiful in such stories.) The Chief had taken it into his head that his daughter would marry a young chieftain of one of the northern tribes who was "quite gallant and had won many honors on the battlefield," thus serving to unite and strengthen the nation. Unfortunately for all, however, the princess had fallen desperately in love with a local warrior of low degree, "what you would call a 'private' in your army, Major!" (At this juncture, it felt like the old chief's tom-tom had started off under my left breast pocket. Had my charade been discovered only to be my undoing with lovely Annie?) Turning toward me, for we had been gazing out over the broad expanse of the Ohio, my hostess concluded her history of our beloved rendezvous.

When the irate Chief learned of his daughter's affections, he bound the young warrior to this very rock and confined the princess to her wigwam, threatening to kill the former if he ever found him near the latter. One moonlit night, both lovers were found missing and legend has it that they cheated the old Chief's tomahawk by taking this scenic, but all too-fatal route to their common destiny. Her story finished, Miss Annie put the key question to me: "Wasn't the Chief a cruel wretch, Major, to threaten the poor fellow's life just because he loved his daughter?"

"I think he was rather hard on him," I replied, "but a private soldier has no business falling in love with a Chief's daughter."

"That's fine, Maje, but no reason a Chief's daughter should not fall in love with a private soldier."[18]

Suddenly the notion came to me that here would be a good place to test the veracity of what Captain Taylor had said on the evening of our first visit to Colonel R's——family, i.e., "You wouldn't fall in love with a private soldier, would you, Miss Annie?"

"Why not, Maje?" she asked, in a tone of some surprise.

"Oh, nothing. I just thought I'd ask the question," I mumbled, turning toward the setting sun whose dying rays were now bathing our outcropping and the beautiful river below. At this point, Miss Annie rose from the smooth ledge we had been using as a settee and came toward me much more serious in her demeanor.

"Val," she said, reaching out to grasp my arm and planting herself between me and the setting sun, "my idle flirtation has ended. You must realize by now that my feelings for you are akin to those of the maid in our story." I tried to blurt out my reciprocal feelings, but a gentle touch of her white-gloved finger to my lips halted that notion. Miss Annie continued, "I have discerned a certain sadness about you despite the many happy and precious moments we have shared since first we met. You escaped an earthly prison to risk your life and liberty to call on me. Now you must loose the bonds around your heart if it is ever to hold for me the bountiful love mine holds for you. I have shown you the way."

Well, "Maje" was struck dumb after that address. Buying time so I could organize my thoughts, I led my companion back to our love seat without speaking. As she seated herself, her face raised expectantly toward mine, it seemed that the entire outcropping of Lover's Leap became instantaneously bathed in scarlet light. I stood transfixed by the unfamiliar, changing hues now cascading across the hill to the river below, no longer simply a masquerading major of Kentucky irregulars. It seemed via all my senses as if this were the setting of Signal Rock on Lookout Mountain a year and a half ago. I was standing, therefore, exactly where I had last seen "Old Pete" up on that promontory, his large frame silhouetted by the red signal flares blazing instructions down to his ill-fated troops at Wauhatchie. Moments later, my own steps had been forced northward on the road to prison, separated it seemed forever from the youthful exhilaration of earlier victories. Slowly, I seated myself next to Annie and unburdened myself of the whole story.

When I finished my tale (which had included no small denunciation of Braxton Bragg as you might have guessed), complete darkness had descended about us. Descended, of course, except for Miss Annie's white shawl, which shimmered about her silhouette like an angel's wings. "Oh, Sarge," she sighed leaning forward to embrace me despite my obvious reduction in rank. "I knew you could do it, just as I was able to tell you earlier of the sadness that enveloped me up at Louisville."

It seems, dear reader, that Annie too had been in a type of bondage during my incarceration at Camp Morton. Her mother had fallen desperately ill and for a full year this faithful daughter had nursed her day and night in a clinic up in Louisville before the lady finally succumbed the same night I escaped from the pesthouse. Subsequently, I had been the only one outside of the immediate family to whom she felt free to unburden herself about this tragedy and this is what she meant when she said, "I have shown you the way."

As we reached the house where candles gleamed from every window, Miss Annie turned and offered me

her kiss. "Now it is clear what we must do, Val. Let us together join in writing the last chapter to your 'Ramblin'
Recollections.' You and I shall reconcile for all who come
after us that awful contradiction between what was and
what might have been in your corps' struggle to hold fast
the gateway into our beloved Southland."

So it is in accordance with Miss Annie's heartfelt
wish that I now offer the final chapter of where the
"Stormy Sixties" would have taken us if Braxton Bragg
had been "Listening to Old Pete" in the fall of '63.

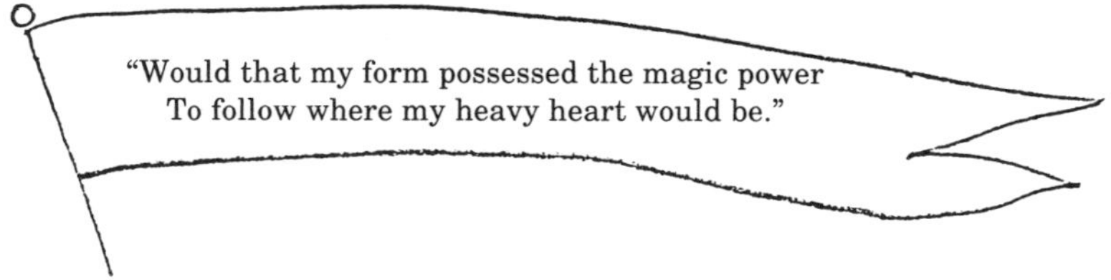

Six

. . . as he carried his slashed red battleflag into the dusky twilight of the Lost Cause, he marched straight into a legend that will live as long as the American people care to remember anything about the American Past.

Catton's *The Confederate Legend*

Scanning Bragg's Bridgeport order a second time, General Longstreet handed it across the makeshift breakfast table to his chief of staff and asked, "Well, Colonel Sorrell, what do you make of this?" After studying the order dated October 15, 1863, the staff officer replied,

It would seem, General, that this order is but a passing reference to the suggestion you gave the President three days ago. According to my minutes of that meeting, the President had agreed with your intention that the better part of this army should cross the river to preempt any threat to its current position. Certainly General Bragg does not expect our 10,000 men to defeat the several armies now converging to lift this siege.

Longstreet raised himself slowly from his seat in front of the large tree stump that had served as a breakfast table that morning. Stretching wide his arms, he appeared to his watching aide as if the body and mind stiffened by the protracted siege was being infused with a fresh air of optimism. With a wan smile, the Commander of the First Corps retrieved Bragg's order from his aide and gently shook it aloft before speaking.

As with most things desirable, Colonel, half-a-loaf is better than none at all. As you know, I have urged in vain for a continuation of offensive operations against the enemy on the opposite bank since we first arrived in this position one month ago. I believed then that the armies hastening to aid General Rosecrans would have been drawn north into defensive positions above the Ohio to halt such a course of action. Subsequently, as I told the President several days ago, the time and resources necessary for the successful execution of such an operation were squandered. Despite this, I remain convinced that even a modest concession to what I earlier proposed could be successful for two reasons.

1. Only General Hooker *or* General Sherman will use Bridgeport for an attack against our left but not both. One of these forces must be directed against our right which severely overlaps the defense of Chattanooga.

2. It is not necessary to completely defeat the enemy force intended for Bridgeport if we can reach that junction first and destroy its capacity to facilitate a crossing of the Tennessee River.

Please inform General McLaws and General Jenkins to meet me here promptly at noon and to ready their divisions for a night march. In the meantime, I will be at General Bragg's headquarters.

At noon, October 15, 1863, Longstreet would return to his headquarters to find his divisional commanders waiting. Lafayette McLaws had been an integral component of First Corps operations who had proven himself in the field and on the march from Fredericksburg to Chattanooga, but Micah Jenkins was untested in his new role as head of Hood's old division. Although the young South Carolinian had assumed command when Hood was incapacitated east of the Brotherton Farm, the circumstances surrounding the confirmation of his promotion were proving to be a festering sore on the morale of the once-famed division the longer Bragg's siege of Chattanooga continued.

According to the historical record referred to above, this festering wound finally burst during Bragg's tantrum-induced reaction to the appearance of Hooker's force on his left at Wauhatchie Station during October 28, 1863. Now, in "Listening to Old Pete," as the president had ordered three days ago, the "ugliest man in the Corps" had finally chosen the wiser alternative of a preemptive strike against Hooker at Bridgeport, Alabama. One week after President Davis's conference with Longstreet, the new Federal Commander of Western Armies dismissed Rosecrans in favor of General Thomas, "the rock of Chickamauga." Ironically, as the limping U.S. Grant turned toward his waiting railroad car in Louisville, Kentucky, he posed the self-same question asked by Longstreet's lieutenants as their conference of war ended at 12:30 P.M. October 15, 1863: "How long will it take us to reach Bridgeport?"

"Gentleman," Longstreet intoned after dismounting and returning the salutes of his subordinates, "your punctuality today must become characteristic of all that is to follow if we are to succeed. There was much to discuss with General Bragg of a logistical nature, but I have reduced all to a five-paragraph order. You will make but one copy of this order utilizing whatever encryption was brought with us from Virginia and guarding same with your life. I see Colonel Sorrell has already placed the map on that stump, so let us begin there.

LONGSTREET'S FIVE-PARAGRAPH ORDER
for the ATTACK against BRIDGEPORT, ALABAMA 15
October
1863

I. <u>Situation:</u> The Federal supply depot at Bridgeport, Alabama twelve miles west of our current position, poses the greatest threat to both the success of the present siege and the future safety of this army. It is from this junction that the majority of foodstuffs and supplies sustaining the enemy garrison in Chattanooga emanate. It will be from this junction that an enemy force will be deployed to shorten that supply line vis-à-vis a concerted attack against our exposed units in Lookout Valley. To forestall that eventuality, First Corps has been assigned a pre-emptive mission which I first proposed to the President three days ago.

II. <u>Mission:</u> The primary mission of First Corps is to launch a pre-emptive attack against the Federal supply depot at Bridgeport, Alabama at approximately 4:30 A.M., October 19th. This part of the mission will include the destruction of all railroad facilities, warehouses and supplies within a one-mile radius of the Tennessee River Bridge crossing. Any counterattack against this primary mission will be sustained as long as is necessary to accomplish our secondary objective: Destruction of the Tennessee River bridge after all units have re-crossed to defensive works on this side of the river. Lastly, these works will be utilized to deny the crossing of any Federal force intended for the relief of Chattanooga vis-à-vis an attack on the left flank of the Army of Tennessee.

III. <u>Execution</u>: The execution of the above mission will proceed as follows:

    A. At 11:00 P.M. this evening, General Jenkins will move his division west along the base of Raccoon Mountain with as much quietude as possible; his present position will be assumed by General McLaws who will repeat this maneuver at 11:00 P.M. October 16th. (General Hardee will occupy our former position once our departure is completed.)

    B. General Jenkins, having secured sufficient rest for his men during the morning hours of the 16th, shall proceed the remaining six miles to the nearest high ground on this side of the river north of the Tennessee River Bridge taking care to arrive after nightfall. Construction of defensive works should begin as soon as his men are nourished and be completed by daybreak; General McLaws will repeat this maneuver having arrived after dark on the 17th to a position south of the Tennessee River Bridge.

    C. Key to the successful execution of the above mission will be the rapid establishment of a bridgehead on the opposite bank of the Tennessee River in Bridgeport itself. This key, gentlemen, will turn only through a close coordination of the following four elements:

        1. The 44th Alabama under Colonel Perry, comprised of officers and men familiar with the Bridgeport area, will be detached by General Jenkins after he is in position to a point on the tracks five miles south of Bridgeport where

they will sequester themselves. At midnight of the 18th, Colonel Perry will rendezvous with

2. A train dispatched this morning from Chickamauga Station with captured Union uniforms and colors.

3. Colonel Perry will outfit his men and the train as if it were a Federal supply unit detached by Sherman for the Bridgeport depot. This representation must be made no later than 4:30 A.M. October 18th to the Federal pickets on this side of the Tennessee River Bridge.

   a. Colonel Perry's presentation to the pickets will be augmented by a squad of General Forrest's cavalry coming up on the train from Chickamauga.

   b. At the time to be determined by Colonel Perry, that the pickets are sufficiently distracted and separated from the train by the cavalry, the train shall proceed with all haste across the bridge halting when the last car has cleared.

   c. The 44th Alabama, having detrained, will endeavor to initiate an assault against all enemy units in a perimeter 150 yards north of the tracks.

   d. The train meanwhile will return to this side of the river securing two regiments designated by each of you to proceed across with the purpose of enlarging the perimeter of operations. All other regiments will follow at the quickstep excepting two left with the bulk of our artillery to staff the trenches on this side of the river in the event of a withdrawal.

e. The immediate results of the successful execution of the above will be to destroy Bridgeport as a staging area for an attack against the Army of Tennessee now besieging Chattanooga and the re-supply of the enemy garrison at that place. All of the above to be completed before noon on October 18th.

IV. <u>Administration:</u>

A. All units shall carry three days rations and sixty rounds of ammunition.

B. Re-supply will be determined by the quartermasters of both divisions from enemy stores captured at Bridgeport. Surplus stores will be shipped back to the defensive works for off-loading after all attacking units have been engaged.

C. General Jenkins' Division will engage the enemy nearest the river to a point 800 yards inland; General McLaws will be responsible for enlarging the perimeter from that point to one 400 yards west of the last structure in the town.

V. <u>Communication:</u>

A. My headquarters will remain on this side of the river with signal corps communication through designated officers of both your attacking divisions.

B. The bridge must remain open for resupply and evacuation of wounded along with hand-delivered orders.

C. A red flare in the possession of General Jenkins is to be utilized if the train itself is disabled; a red flare from my headquarters will signal a general withdrawal across the bridge.

—Gentlemen, are there any questions?

*　　*　　*

It might be instructive at this point to pause for the purpose of determining what the most immediate effects of the Bridgeport Order would be on the historical record of the Chattanooga campaign. It also might be instructive to assume that the most immediate effects on this record would be the most obvious ones. Alternative history is weakened the further it moves from the immediate and obvious into the broader field of speculation. Even allowing for the complete failure of what Longstreet above called the "key" to his order—establishment of a bridgehead in Bridgeport by an entrained regiment of Alabamians—the immediate effects of placing the First Corps in defensive works opposite a destroyed Tennessee River Bridge would produce the following obvious consequences:

1. Hooker could <u>NOT</u> have crossed the Tennessee River Bridge to suddenly appear on Bragg's left in Lookout Valley on October 28, 1863.
2. There could <u>NOT</u> have been a Battle of Wauhatchie on October 28, 1863, insuring a shortened "cracker line" for the besieged Federals via Brown's Ferry (despite what General Grant and Smith had planned.) Therefore,
3. U. S. Grant could <u>NOT</u> have boasted as he did "that within (7) days of his arrival in Chattanooga the way was open . . . and the men were receiving full rations."[1]
4. Consequently, U. S. Grant would be forced by # 1-3 to develop an alternate strategy for lifting the siege of Chattanooga.

I believe the first three consequences of Longstreet's

153

Bridgeport alternative to be "airtight." They can be agreed to as logical effects of such a move by both casual readers of the Chattanooga campaign and serious historians alike. It should also be obvious to all, however, that this particular analysis of alternative history would enter the field of speculation if it sought to determine what exactly U. S. Grant would have done to counter a Confederate investment of Bridgeport. This is *not* to say that historians are eternally forbidden from entering the field of historical speculation. Indeed, if the scientific analysis of our physical world proceeds from time-to-time along lines of "probability," certainly the social scientist should be allowed to travel within similar parameters when necessity dictates. The necessity for providing a complete accounting of how "Listening to Old Pete" altered the record of the Chattanooga campaign dictates that we now mark clearly the parameters of analyzing Grant's reactions to the execution of the Bridgeport order. This we can do by stringing lower-case sub-points clearly marked "probably" from the farthest-most boundary of the historical record, i.e.

1. Grant "probably" would have retained Hooker's original deployment to Bridgeport, Alabama, as per the historical record. This supply depot was too vital in sustaining the Federal hold on Chattanooga still viewed by the leadership of both North and South as the "gateway" into Georgia and the Deep South. Hooker now, however, would "probably" be ordered to drive out the rebels.
2. Grant "probably" would have retained Sherman's original deployment to Chattanooga as ordered in the historical record. More than any other general, Grant felt Sherman was the key to breaking Bragg's siege.

The historical record before and after Grant's arrival had convinced him that without Sherman's veterans, the demoralized Army of the Cumberland " . . . could not get out of their trenches to assume the offensive."[2]
3. Grant "probably" would have redeployed Burnside's Army to provide both an alternate supply line and the manpower denied him by Hooker's engagement at Bridgeport.

One of the best hedges against the inherent dangers of historical speculation are the primary accounts of the ordinary people who lived during the particular time period. Unlike political or military leaders who write their memoirs with one eye on their desired place in history, there is less proselytizing or ax-grinding in the daily diaries and letters of those who fail to qualify for the "great man" theory of historiography. Ironically, however, it is from these same primary accounts of the disenfranchised that the lifeblood of history flows. We would search Grant's or Longstreet's memoirs a long time for anything other than a self- justification for macro-cosmic actions taken or denunciations for others ignored by their immediate superiors or subalterns. Yet in the simple compact between a Texas sergeant and his Kentucky sweetheart, we are given a rare vehicle through which to follow the Bridgeport order clothed in the flesh and blood of "ordinary" people. Through the last chapter of his "Ramblin' Recollections," we can follow the steps of Val Giles "to where his heavy heart would be"—with the last First Corps offensive in the fall of '63.

*   *   *

As the saying goes, dear reader, "mighty oaks from

little acorns grow." The resumption of offensive operations by the First Corps and our welcome detachment from Bragg's interminable siege of Chattanooga had humble beginnings. The Fourth Texas Regiment had no sooner stepped off as the vanguard on this auspicious occasion before we discovered that someone had forgotten to replace the planks on the two bridges across Lookout Creek. I know for a fact that Jenkins's entire division crossed over on the stringers like four silent lines of tight-rope walkers. I know this because it was yours truly who was detailed to backtrack and inform General McLaws to bring forward planking for the artillery the following night. Despite the lieutenant's faith in my long legs, it was getting on toward 1 A.M. before I got back to the crossing point. Falling in with the last of the rear guard, I heel-to-toed it across the stringers using my Enfield as a balance bar, convincing myself all the while that if one could travel faster than thousands, it wouldn't take long to catch up to my regiment on its line of march along the eastern base of Raccoon Mountain.

Just as I began to split moonbeams on the side of the now-congested roadway, however, a grave sense of melancholia wept over me as I passed through Wauhatchie. To this day my only explanation for this feeling was that I was suddenly cut-off from the view of the strangely-silent columns to my left by a heavy stand of pines.

At any rate, the feeling passed as my comrades once more came into view and my fevered brow refreshed by a sudden breeze off the river. According to Lieutenant Hays who had detached me as a messenger, it was around 2:30 A.M. when I caught up to old Company B as it drew opposite Williams Island. Although our unit was getting progressively louder the further it got from Chattanooga—here about four miles—my eyes proved more useful than my ears in finding company headquarters and reporting my mission completed.

Intellectually there was no finer company commander in the entire brigade than Captain B. F. Carter of Company B. He exhibited the finest combination of a well-trained legal mind with that of a natural-born soldier, manifesting itself in a strict discipline grounded in fairness and practicality. His special gift was the ability to impart every nuance of Hardee's *Tactics* "so thoroughly that the biggest blockhead in the ranks could understand them."[3] On a long march, however, Captain Carter's physical limitations became obvious to all. On occasions such as this, I looked for his supportive retinue that had divided up its commander's gear amongst themselves. Lieutenant Hays habitually carried the Captain's sword and belt while three enlisted men took his haversack, canteen and bedroll. The men who increased their load for Captain Carter on their way to battle were merely paying homage to a man who had taught them to dance well to the music of many bullets once the battle was joined. As I turned to rejoin my squad, his parting words came through labored breath, "Well done, sergeant. We are more than halfway to the first resting point."

At daybreak our column halted, moved off the road a considerable distance and cooked breakfast. The news that we were to remain concealed in this place until nightfall, coupled with my recent exertions, resulted in the soundest sleep I had experienced since the start of the Chattanooga campaign. I was awakened around midday by the raucous passage through our campsite of three Alabamians. They made it clear that being familiar with the Bridgeport neighborhood, they had been ordered forward to scout the location of Yankee pickets on this side of the Tennessee River Bridge. They would then rendezvous with our column when it reached a point three miles from the crossing. Although their trek would involve more mileage than I had covered backtracking Lookout Mountain for General McLaws, these Alabamians would have close to nine hours and the company of comrades to lighten their journey. Having thus justified my intentions for a relaxing afternoon, I folded my bedroll and joined other members of my squad for a repast of salt bacon and roasted ears of Tennessee corn. I reckon we started looking too relaxed because Lieutenant Hays stopped by in short order to give us a strategy session on the role our company would play once we got opposite Bridgeport. He sure tested our digestion when he left us with the admonition to save our strength for the digging that lay ahead. This turned out to be sound advice.

Our column, which took to the road after nightfall on October 16th, arrived in the vicinity of Bridgeport just before midnight. As luck would have it, my squad had been assigned to patrol the regimental right flank about three hours back, so my trip west would end as it began—about one hundred yards to the right of the main line of march. It was from this position that my squad and I came close to firing on General Longstreet himself along with his officer of engineers. This near-calamitous mishap occurred in the following way.

About the time I had made the determination that Bridgeport was less than one mile away due to a faint glow against the western sky, the sound of marching feet off to our left ceased completely and all went silent. Waiting for at least three of the six men patrolling behind me to come up, we agreed it would be best to consolidate the squad and move forward with utmost caution. If necessary, one man could be dispatched over to the main column to ascertain the reason for the halt. We had no sooner resumed our forward movement in execution of this plan than the distinct sound of horses and muffled voices seemed to arise out of the ground to our front. Without command, my squad placed their Enfields on full cock and went prone. Slowly inching ourselves forward in a firing line, we came to the embankment of a sunken road running across our immediate front. Here, two figures on horseback were moving slowly northward preceded by two infantrymen. I could have spit green hornets when young Billy Richards gave us away by calling out, "Let's take 'em, Sarge!" The two horsemen reined in immediately and the infantrymen sped right under our embankment and out of sight much less shooting range. I reckoned all Hades was about to break loose as three of my men jumped to their feet to get these foot soldiers into their line of fire. Instantaneously, however, this chaotic scene froze as if in a picture when the largest of the two horsemen raised his hand palm upward like a preacher at a prayer meeting and intoned, "Boys, if you're Yankees there is a full Confederate division on the road between you and Bridgeport. If you are who I think you are, though, come forward and assist us." It was Old Pete himself and we scrambled down the embankment as he directed.

As it turned out, my small squad gave no small assistance in providing the groundwork for General Longstreet's Bridgeport alternative. The two riflemen in his lead party were the same Alabamians who had gone through our camp earlier to conduct a reconnaissance of the ground on this side of the Tennessee River Bridge. Apparently they had convinced General Longstreet that this sunken ferry road, which paralleled the river from an abandoned landing opposite Bridgeport, would provide excellent concealment for our two divisions during the daylight hours. To this end, their third companion had already been sent back to the main road to guide Evander Law's Brigade south along the sunken road to prepare trenches for McLaw's Division, which was to arrive at this time next evening. (Such preparation might serve the double purpose of quashing McLaw's complaint that our division had left him with bridge-building duties back at Lookout Creek!) The only fly in this ointment was that the three Alabamian scouts were part of Colonel Perry's Forty-fourth Regiment that was to rendezvous with the "assault" train three miles south of the crossing. The discussion my squad had overheard was whether the two men now accompanying Old Pete to mark the extreme right of our division could backtrack in time to make this important rendezvous. It had been understood from the beginning that the men of the Forty-fourth Alabama were to be spared all trench-digging duties and this is where the sudden appearance of my squad came in handy. Immediately the two riflemen were dispatched back along the sunken road with instructions to notify Jenkins to enter it and proceed to the point my squad would mark as the extreme right of our defensive line opposite Bridgeport.

In this manner, two trenches were to be opened on the night of October 16th running toward one another from points one-half mile south and one-half north of the Tennessee River Bridge. This plan was necessitated by the reported presence of a three-squad Yankee picket posted at the junction of the main road and the bridge. Apparently their bonfire whose light I had seen earlier, would be extinguished at the first sign that danger was afoot. With the moonlit form of General Longstreet silently leading the way, we followed that old sunken road paralleling the sparkling Tennessee convinced that both were leading us to victory.

Although the excitable Billy Richards had been given a shovel by one of the departing Alabamians, my squad's spirits peaked even further when the engineering officer revealed he had packed along only one additional shovel and pick for the initiation of our ground-breaking duties. This officer had halted our band after a half-mile was covered and climbed up the embankment and out of view with Old Pete close behind.

After a short confab, they summoned us up and over to start the trench line about twenty-five yards nearer the river. This locale had a commanding view of the Bridge-port crossing but was not immediately visible to the Yankee picket on our side due to a significant rise in the land to our left. After promising us immediate relief when the rest of our division joined us and with a strict admonition against building any fires, General Longstreet and his engineer mounted and rode silently back toward the main road to check on the progress of Law's Brigade. They were gone but a short while before we heard the approach of our division and the sunken road behind us began filling up with the familiar forms of the old Texas Brigade.

I would be hard-put to determine the most raucous day ever spent in the Confederate Army during the "Stormy Sixties." There were certainly many of those in camp, on the march and in the heat of the aftermath of battle. The one singular quietest day I ever spent, however, stands out like a Baptist minister in a barroom brawl—it was October 17, 1863. All digging stopped an hour before sunrise when all personnel returned to the sunken road. Loud talk, guffaws and generally all back-slapping behavior were strictly forbidden along with the previous night's admonition against building campfires. Even the most necessary of orders were given in hushed whispers so as not to alert the Yankee pickets who were still out of sight, but yet a mere one thousand yards, as I guessed it, from our sequestered position. Meanwhile, utmost care had been taken to remove all earth dislodged from the trench site to the sunken road to prevent it from being spotted by field-glasses over in Bridgeport. So here you have the complete picture of Jenkins's Division on the eve of what came to be called the Battle of Bridgeport Station: a sizable number of mute Confederate staring at one another while consuming a cold breakfast seated in a sunken road on shifting piles of dislodged trench dirt. Granted, not a pretty picture at first glance, but it had some saving graces. First off, once our cold repast was downed, concerted attention was turned to the care and cleaning of all personal accouterments. Rifles were cleaned and recleaned, all pouches were checked for the requisite sixty rounds and faulty shoe leather was repaired in preparation for the healthy sprint that lay ahead. Lastly, even the most menial of boredom-busting assignments found ready volunteers. While some set block and tackle in preparation for hauling dismounted Napoleons out of the sunken road, yours truly volunteered his squad to scout the rest of the sunken road to the north of our position since it bent out of sight down toward the abandoned ferry landing. "Giles," Lieutenant Hays whispered as I gathered my men together, "we figure Colonel Alexander could use some planking for the guns when they get here, but don't take any unnecessary chances of getting spotted."

As we rounded the bend in the road and dropped from the sight of our silent encampment, the boys started to loosen up considerably. Again, the chief interlocutor was young Billy Richards, who had come up as a replacement from Texas after the battle around the Brotherton Farm. Thanks to the subsequent strategy adopted by General Bragg, this private had never fired a shot in anger or been fired at as far as I knew. Whether this was a factor in explaining his boisterousness or not, I had no time to determine. The Tennessee River was now clearly visible through the fall foliage a quarter-mile ahead. If six raucous "graybacks" came down to the water's edge like a bunch of truant schoolboys, it could well ruin any chances of taking the Yankees by surprise the next morning. Halting my now-carefree band, I reimpressed them with the need for stealth and silence. Our major objective was to determine if the old ferrylanding could be used by the enemy to outflank our trench-line being built several hundred yards to the south.

Secondarily, I was determined to secure any planks or rails, which habitually seem to inhabit deserted and active ferry sites alike. Placing three men at wide-depth intervals on the right side of the road, I instructed them to follow the last man of the three separated in like manner on the left side. With Billy walking point in this latter group and me close enough behind him to read the print on his cartridge box, we started forward again. As we got within thirty feet of the water's edge, it became obvious to all that the ferry landing could not accommodate even the most modest attempt at landing troops.

The landing itself was but thirty-feet wide, muddied out and bordered by steep, slippery banks. More to the point, out in the river just opposite the landing, considerable flotsam could be observed, a greater part of which was the turned-over hulk of what must have been the last ferry across the Tennessee at this point. This debris was causing an angry mix of whirl-pools and sucks that would wreak havoc on any craft seeking to marry-up with the landing from the Bridgeport side of the river. The attending good news was that a sizable amount of planking for repairs and fence rails for the penning of animals were piled to the right of the landing. When we reported back to Lieutenant Hays a short time later, however, we were chastised for not bringing some of these planks with us, but I convinced this officer that such work was best left for sundown since both the site and work crew could conceivably be observed by glasses from the opposite bank.

After a hearty but cold supper, the bulk of the above work was carried out by a sizable contingent from the Eighth Georgia, which, along with the Seventh, had been designated to stay behind and man the trenches during our attack against Bridgeport in the morning. Their plank-hauling duties were completed just as the muffled sounds of Colonel Alexander's approaching artillery greeted our ears. Without skipping a beat, this officer proceeded to detail ten Georgia boys apiece to haul the cannon out of the sunken road come daylight. The men of the Fourth Texas opined more than once that night to both artillerists and goober alike how fighting was preferable to the manual labor awaiting those who stayed behind on this side of the Tennessee. As the wheels of each artillery piece ground to a halt in front of the position it would occupy in the morning, all could hear the tred of McLaws's Division filing into the sunken road to the south of the Bridgeport pike.

We were awakened about two hours before sunrise on the 18th of October to a cold drizzle and some last-minute instructions for the attack against Bridgeport. Whether the train bearing the Forty-fourth Alabama came up or not, neither Robertson's nor Bennings's Brigades would be issued any tickets for the ride across the

Tennessee River Bridge. Since both these units had entered the sunken road first, they were now furthest from the tracks and would therefore proceed down to the bridge via the hill to their front. Meanwhile, Law's and Anderson's Brigades would fill up the first three cars of the returning train via their closer placement to the main road, which led down to the bridge. The last three boxcars were reserved for two of General McLaw's Brigades (or as many as could squeeze into the dilapidated rolling stock of the Confederacy in the fall of '63). Again, failing the appearance of the train, the whole plan would devolve upon the last-mentioned units surprising the Yankee picket on this side and leading a divisional footrace across the Tennessee River Bridge before the sounds of reveille. The desperation of this contingency became evident to all the minute Captain Carter finished explaining it. As providence would have it, however (as providence was widely-implored) the sounds of an approaching locomotive soon punctuated the drenched solemnity of our morning meal. The Forty-fourth Alabama had come up with the wayward train from Chickamauga!

Dawn was more than an hour away and the troops at our end of the sunken road were forced to rely on sketchy reports by two officers who had crawled forward of the trench line with field-glasses. Through the uncertain images coming up to these men from the dancing glare of the picket's bonfire merged against the steady beam of the locomotive's headlamp, many eager ears were strained toward those officers to piece together the first chapter in the Battle of Bridgeport Station.

It seems the Yankee pickets had been more curious than alarmed at the appearance of a train chugging up to their post an hour before reveille with Union banners flying. A figure wearing the uniform of a Union officer had swung out of the cab to engage the officer of the picket in conversation. Lieutenant Hays even called back softly that the figure looked like Colonel Perry himself, pulling off what must have been the major masquerade of his life. Meanwhile, a half-dozen horsemen in Yankee caps were reported ranging along the first three cars of the train and we hoped against hope that these were Forrest's men loaned to our expedition. From that point on, things quickly started to unravel. Apparently the officer Colonel Perry had engaged in conversation, turned and directed three of his men up onto the bridge leading over to Bridgeport, while the train, steam up, remained in-place. It was anybody's guess as to whether he was merely following protocol or had made an independent decision to notify the garrison. From what he did next, it was apparent Colonel Perry figured it didn't make much difference if the element of surprise was to be lost. With a sudden effusion of steam and screeching steel that cascaded over our hidden position, the train started over the Tennessee River Bridge as our two interlocutors quickly returned to their commands in the sunken road. The Battle of Bridgeport had begun!

As we scrambled out of the sunken road to form up below the trenchline for our dash across the bridge, the sonorous echo of rifle fire across the river valley announced Colonel Perry's arrival in Bridgeport. Soon, the rebel yell could be heard on both sides of the Tennessee as the Brigades of Law and Anderson wildly raced those from McLaws's Division down to the now-subdued picket post from which Forrest's men were herding our first prisoners. Moving down the hill with a more measured cadence, our brigade actually beheld the hurtling caboose of the returning train before the jubilant winners of the footrace who seemed to have momentarily forgotten that a more important contest lay ahead.

Finally, with four brigades of graybacks swarming in and over her, the old puff-belly gathered steam for the second run across. The unlucky ones who were bumped for a place began to quick-step it along the narrow catwalks on either side of the tracks, issuing a few healthy oaths back toward their luckier comrades. It became apparent, however, that the former group would have to inhale considerably when the boxcars of protruding bodies passed if they were to avoid being knocked into the Tennessee River like the three Yankee pickets before them. Despite the chaos of the unfolding scene, I could not help but be reminded of our First Corps train ride from Virginia only one month ago. If the Yankee cracker line could be broken by this attack and Lookout Valley sealed against a Yankee incursion, we could still succeed in pulling Bragg's chestnuts from the fire. Cheers went along our ranks as General Longstreet galloped past to confer with the divisional commanders who were viewing the train's shaky return to Bridgeport through their fieldglasses.

Suddenly, these cheers were punctuated by a rising crescendo of rifle fire that seemed to erupt from the side of the train just as it cleared the bridge. Passing the officers' conference, we overheard General Jenkins opine that the advance brigades had opened fire in support of Colonel Perry's men before the train had even come to a halt. We had been instructed to break our sprint across the bridge into thirds. With McLaws's men on the left, we were to double-time it, follow up with a quick walk and conclude with a double-time sprint into a position east of the station. McLaws's boys griped they had it rougher since they had to go past the station and extend the salient out to the west of town. Under the watchful eye of its commander the Texas Brigade began pounding the planks in what turned out to be its last offensive operation in the western theater.

I was a gangly twenty-one-year-old at this time, a mite over six feet. There was no doubt in my mind that I could complete this dash across the Tennessee River Bridge and still have enough steam to engage the Yankees on the other side. Mere words can not describe my exhilaration at being released from the inertia of a month-long siege to move out against the Yankees in company with my cheering, grunting and cursing comrades of the Fourth Texas. My only concern as our steps reverberated along those wooden planks like a herd of wild mustangs was for the condition of our company commander, Captain Carter. Lieutenant Hays had just stepped out from the column to check back for any stragglers and the Captain's sword and belt were clearly visible hanging over his shoulder as was customary during a hard march.

Glancing over my shoulder, I saw the captain far to the rear staggering precariously in the middle of the tracks where the widely-separated ties made for treacherous footing. It looked certain that Company B would have to begin this battle without its company commander, but help soon arrived from an unexpected quarter. Although we had been specifically instructed on how to deport ourselves if the train started back over with captured stores, the rear cars now came slowly rolling toward us just as we were gearing up for our final sprint. The movement of the cars seemed so slow and purposeful, however, few of us took the precautionary position next to the side railings as we had been instructed. Suddenly, an officer in blue emerged from the back door of the caboose

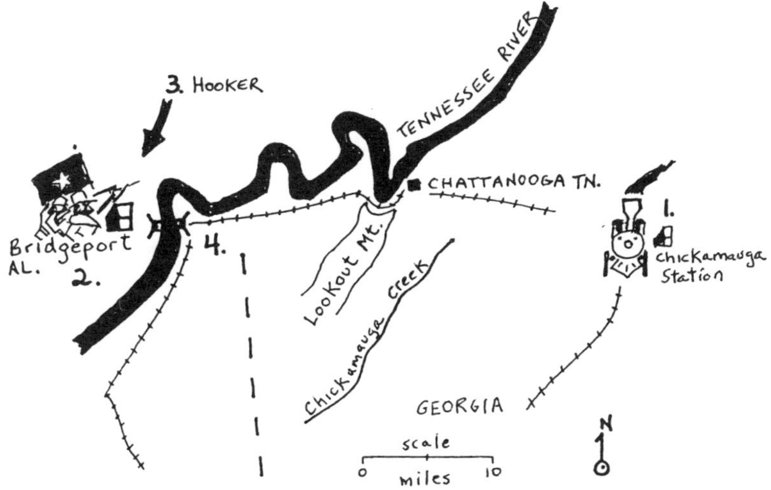

The Map above shows the theater of operations for General Longstreet's
two divisions during the Bridgeport (Alabama) Campaign, October 18-25, 1863:
1. A train bearing captured Union accoutrements and a cavalry detachment
is dispatched from Chickamaugua Station on October 15th. 2. After this train
is used by the 44th Alabama to establish a bridgehead in Bridgeport at
dawn on October 18th, the divisions of Jenkins and McLaws move across the
Tennessee River Bridge to subdue the garrison. 3. Union General Hooker,
whose army Grant had intended to use in shortening the "cracker line" and
attacking Bragg's left on Lookout Mountain, arrives at Bridgeport on
October 25th to find its' facilities destroyed and two entrenched Confederate
divisions. 4. After battling Hooker's superior force, Longstreet's men
withdraw to prepared positions on the opposite bank of the Tennessee River
having destroyed the bridge and Grant's plans for Hooker in lifting the siege
of Chattanooga.

and calmly addressed the gaping rebels as the cars moved slowly by in the direction of Captain Carter, "Gentlemen, let it never be said that the sovereign state of Alabama forced her defenders to run to her aid. Climb aboard and we'll go in style." Immediately three huzzahs went up for Colonel Perry of the Forty-fourth Alabama, and those who were unwilling or unable to accept his gracious invitation, found themselves loading a barrel or two of Yankee contraband when they finally reached the station moments later.

As we formed up to the right of the station, it was obvious the Yankees had been caught by surprise. Colonel Perry's regiment had hit this point before reveille since the familiar notes never reached our ears on the other side. Triple rows of riddled and torn canvas did little to cover the bloodied corpses of half-clothed men killed during the pre-dawn attack. Blankets and ticking strewn away from us showed the desperate flight of those who lay but a few yards north of their last earthly repose. Except for the one near the end of the platform, around which lay the fully-clothed bodies of a few pickets, it was evident that no breakfast fires had been started in the encampment before us.

Meanwhile, the Brigades of Law and Anderson had pushed the enemy to our front about four hundred yards north of the tracks where they had taken up a defensive position in a large redan flanked by a deep trench filled with bluecoats on either side. This trench was anchored nearest the river to a large warehouse from which emanated the measured fire of sharpshooters who were exacting a high toll from the right flank of Anderson's attacking formation. It would be the role of Company B to silence this position of sharpshooters preparatory to an envelopment of the trench by the rest of the Fourth

Texas. Captain Carter strolled right up to yours truly and looked me in the eye. "Sergeant Giles," he said, "there are four hundred yards between us and those sharpshooters. Your squad is a sprightly bunch, but you can't outdodge those Spencers over that distance. Move forward with that bale wagon, keeping your squad to the river side and when you've got their attention, me and the rest of the boys will join you."

With Billy Richards grabbing the tongue as steersman and the rest of us pushing on the outboard side of the aforementioned bale wagon, we moved out rear-end first at an oblique angle to the warehouse. We immediately came under fire from the Yankee sharpshooters who divined that their best chance of stopping our strange advance was to skip their shots under the wagon at our exposed legs. This type of dance music, however, only served to speed up our steps and it was only after we reached our destination that I discovered a sizable splinter from one of the wheel spokes sticking out of my lower left leg. It wasn't the first or last time that the excitement of battle would serve as an opiate to personal injury. We halted the wagon at the extreme southeast corner of the warehouse and without any instruction from me, our squad directed a concerted fire at the hatches, doors and windows along the front of the building. The way I'll always picture it was Billy taking a kneeling position behind the tongue of the wagon since he was a lefty anyway.

Two of the boys got up into the wagon right and left of the topmost bale knocking the one behind them to the ground so they had some space to work their ramrods. The corporal and I went prone to the left and right of this grounded bale while the other two men alternated firing from a standing position behind the back corner of the wagon. Soon the throaty roar of our Enfields and the sharp reports coming from the warehouse obliterated any sense of sound emanating from the general attack against the redan to our left. The corporal and I concentrated on the upper left window, which, being near the end of the building, revealed a similar opening toward the west. Any figure who appeared at the former opening was clearly silhouetted against the blue sky visible through the latter. Thus, by directing our fire through these two openings, we were not only covering the imminent advance of our own company, but also limiting the losses to Anderson's Brigade attacking the redan on the west side of the warehouse.

Just as we reached the halfway mark in our supply of cartridges, Captain Carter thankfully released the rest of our company against the warehouse. We had drawn so much of the enemy's attention toward our position on the southeast corner of the building, that this sudden frontal assault carried some of the more hearty souls right up to the covered loading dock where they commenced pounding the double doors with their rifle butts, calling out for the Yankees inside to surrender. As I jumped to my feet to share in the immediate fruits of our attack, however, a sharp, throbbing pain in my lower left leg brought me down on the grounded bale and it was only then that I saw the sizable splinter protruding from my leg and the clotted blood which had collected around it.

"Take care of that wound, Giles," huffed Captain Carter as he labored up to our mobile redoubt. "Your squad has done its fair share today and me and the boys can take it from here." When I professed my squad's ability to continue, the captain nodded to a line of bluecoat prisoners now emerging from the warehouse with their wounded. "If you would like to be of further service, sergeant, have your men escort those prisoners back to the

station. The provost will take them from you and I believe
a surgeon can be found about the premises."

Using a discarded Yankee Springfield as a cane, I accompanied my prisoner detail back to the station where
the provost guard had designated several boxcars as a
temporary guardhouse. I never did get to see a surgeon
because just then the course of battle and Billy's subsequent discovery of a barrel of cucumbers changed all
things for the better. Returning to the north side of the
station platform, my squad was treated to the panorama
of our Bridgeport incursion in all its final glory. Company
B, now fully ensconced in and about the newly-liberated
warehouse, was pouring a withering fire down the trench
line it had formerly served to anchor. This fire was crowd-
ing the Yankees in the trench toward the redan where the
star-crossed banners of Anderson's Brigade could be seen
mounting the south wall through the haze of battle
smoke. Just as I was about to seat myself on the platform
in deference to my now-benumbed leg, a sharp order from
the other side of the station brought forth the remaining
companies of the Fourth Texas directed toward the confused Yankees who were scrambling over one another to
reach the redan. In short order this phase of the battle
was over and white flags began to appear along the earthworks to our front. Suddenly there was a loud bang behind me and a wave of brine cascaded over my body and
those of my fellow onlookers. It seems Billy, who had
climbed atop a barrel to command a better view of the
battle, had slipped in his excitement and scattered pick-
led cucumbers all over our end of the station platform. My
immediate intent to admonish his carelessness was post-
poned by Billy sliding over to me with the surrender flag
relinquished by our prisoners along with some sage medical advice for my wound. i.e., "Sarge," I recall him ex-

claiming excitedly, "you don't need no doctor. My grandma used pickled-brine compresses to cure everything from warts to blood infections. Let's say we give it a try on your leg."

Well, with that—I can only guess that the sense of victory had superseded my common sense—I allowed Billy to first wash my wound and then dress it with pickle brine and that white Yankee muslin. In between, the boys had a howl at my wild dance and cusses directed at our young nurse-in-training. To tell you the truth though, this oft-repeated treatment coupled with the joyous celebration that swept First Corps that night, did wonders to restore me to full duty by the twenty-first of October. Long after the war was over, however, I could still predict heavy rains and Texas tornadoes by two days via the throbbing in that purplish round scar that was a souvenir of our initial attack at Bridgeport Station.

The next day, although still a joyous one for our troops on both sides of the river, was given over to a more serious assessment of our situation by the officer corps. General Longstreet had set up headquarters in a house near the center of Bridgeport, but the station where General Jenkins was headquartered still served as the nexus of activity and reports connecting the town with our now-completed defensive works on the other side of the river.

The first point of agreement coming down the grapevine telegraph was that our attack had occurred before the anticipated reinforcements intended for Chattanooga had arrived at this place. The quick success of our assault had been based not only on the element of surprise, but, as far as could be determined, a superiority in the number of infantry units engaged. Having pushed to the northern outskirts of town on the 18th, McLaws's Division had observed several Yankee support units, presumably their headquarters, departing hastily on a northbound train during the concluding phases of our raid. How far these units would have to travel before meeting up with the reinforcements for Rosecrans could not be determined. The only scouts that we could rely on in this regard was the small cavalry detachment from Forrest, which was now thinly deployed two miles north of the rail center.

A determination was made by our officer corps, therefore, to improve on existing defensive works so as to contest any counterattack from the north and to speed as many captured enemy supplies as practical over to our works on the east side of the river in the event the town could not be held. With this eventuality in mind, all major facilities were set with explosive charges and wrecking crews were sent out on the tracks for a distance of two miles north and south (toward Stevenson, Alabama) during the next three days. Meanwhile the last train dispatched south from Bridgeport was the one headed for Andersonville, Georgia, with our contribution of Yankee prisoners. The first phase of the Battle of Bridgeport Station was over.

Our communication with Bragg's Army remained with those signal stations First Corps had established along the route we had just taken from Lookout Mountain. Less than a week after our success at Bridgeport, word arrived that Grant had been spotted in Chattanooga. If the "hero of Fort Donelson" had planned to use Bridgeport as a staging area for an attack against the Army of Tennessee, those plans would have to be changed. Apparently, the injured Grant had been carried, pushed and pulled over the carcass-strewn "cracker line" along the north bank of the Tennessee, so he probably knew first-hand that our seizure of the cracker barrel itself posed a bigger threat to his plans than those languid forms arrayed along the top of Missionary Ridge. Confirmation that both Sherman and Halleck had arrived at a similar conclusion arrived providentially during the early morning hours of October 25, 1863.

We had renamed the island in front of Bridgeport "Hood's Island" in honor of our convalescing divisional commander. From this spot on the morning of October 25th, several of our pickets intercepted a Union courier rowing down the Tennessee with a message from Grant destined for Sherman somewhere in northeastern Mississippi. This message decried both Halleck's order that Sherman rebuild the Memphis and Charleston Railroad as well as Sherman's belief that miles of supply wagons would be needed to feed and resupply the Chattanooga garrison. Comparing Grant's obvious disdain for Sherman's supply trains with the latter's distance from Chattanooga, our officers concluded that Grant would soon try to retake Bridgeport with the only troops immediately available for the task—"Fighting Joe" Hooker's contingent from our old adversary, The Army of the Potomac.

They were not long in coming. By sundown on the 25th of October, Forrest's troopers were coming in with news of Yankee columns detraining at the broken rail line two miles north of town. Although the grapevine telegraph had placed Hooker's strength at 20,000 few in the Texas Brigade doubted that he could be checkmated. During the intervening week, all of us had been schooled in the likely outcome of the coming battle: i.e., Hooker would march into the ruins of Bridgeport having paid a high price for the privilege of viewing a heavily-entrenched First Corps on the opposite side of an unfordable river. There would be no crackers for Chattanooga and no bluecoats storming Lookout Mountain if these were Grant's objectives in sending Hooker to Bridgeport.

Robertson's Brigade had been assigned the trench line running east from the redan to the edge of the bluff overlooking the Tennessee River. This position included the warehouse captured by our company one week ago, but as a potential reference point for enemy artillery, only our ablest sharpshooters were placed in sandbagged positions near the building's foundation. The main part of Company B occupied a new trench running about one-hundred yards east of the warehouse right up to the edge of the river bluff. Colonel Alexander had placed three captured artillery pieces in this position whose fields of fire would overlap with three pieces placed to the west of the warehouse. This placement, the gun crews told us, was to discourage any flanking maneuver toward the river, which would threaten the main body of Jenkins's Division defending the redan in the center of the line. It was determined in advance that these pieces would be spiked at the appropriate time rather than removed across the river where most of our artillery waited. The plan was to hold this position commanding the bridge approach until McLaws's Division had been withdrawn behind us. Having removed all the supplies practicable in the past week, two locomotives were brought up behind the station to aid in the re-deployment of our troops to the other side of the Tennessee.

Captain Carter was blunt enough to admit that the success of this stage rested heavily on the assumption that Hooker wouldn't turn his artillery on the bridge itself. Destruction of the Tennessee River Bridge was to be left to our engineers who were to touch off two barrels of Yankee black powder placed in the middle of the span once all our men had re-crossed. At midnight, the torch was set to all structures north and west of our position that might provide cover for the enemy. Adding to the conflagration were the supplies and ordinance that had not been transported to the east side of the river. These signs and sounds must have goaded "Fighting Joe" forward, for his battle formations began appearing through the smoky haze promptly at sunrise of the 26th of October. The third phase in the Battle of Bridgeport Station was about to begin.

From the outset, it was apparent that Hooker's first obstacles would be the numerous smoldering ruins to our front. Where some individual regiments simply halted before these ruins to await orders, others seems to divide almost automatically going around both sides at once. Meanwhile, some regimental officers on horseback sought to lead their entire command intact around one particular side or the other, shouting vehemently at subalterns who failed to divine their purpose. It was at this point that Colonel Alexander's order to fire rang out over the trenchline and the batteries of captured Napoleons opened up as one. Through gaps in the heavy smoke created by brisk river breezes, we saw the disorganized advance to our front turn into a chaotic rush to the rear. The enveloping artillery fire from the left and right of the warehouse exacted a heavy toll on "Fighting Joe's" initial rashness. As yet our infantry had not delivered any volley, although I was aware of some sporadic firing over on our left. Several eager regiments nearer the redan even rushed forward, believing a counterattack was in order. They must have found the Yankees still in some strength beyond the smoldering ruins, for these regiments were quickly recalled to the trenches after engaging in a vigorous skirmish. Company B, as I intimated, was a mere spectator of these developments since we had been ordered to support the artillery pieces to the river-side of the warehouse. Nervous jokes moved along the line to the effect that "Fighting Joe" would have to change his tactics if he wanted to retake Bridgeport before winter.

By noon, Hooker's second attempt to retake Bridgeport commenced. Moving what looked like his entire complement of artillery between the ruins that had earlier broken up his lines of infantry, he commenced such an awful pounding of our entrenched position, that our "contraband" batteries were soon silenced. This Yankee artillery was supported by one division of Howard's XI Corps arranged in three attack columns visible behind the ruins to our left, right and center. To those who cared to hazard a guess amidst the waves of earth, rocks and shells, which hurtled over their prostrate forms, it appeared as if this cannonade was preparatory to an infantry attack by columns against our division. Such was not the case, however, as we were soon to discover. As the rushed order to fix bayonets went down the line, a thunderclap of musketry commenced over to the west.

We learned later that Hooker had swung three other divisions over to engage General McLaws who lacked the luxury of our heavily-entrenched position. By mid-afternoon, McLaws's heavily-outnumbered division was being pushed grudgingly back into town on either side of the tracks. About five hundred yards west of the station house, Old Pete had ordered a second defensive line for McLaw's Division during our week of occupation. Along a siding running at right angles to the line along with this unit was withdrawing, two rows of boxcars had been derailed to rest on their sides along an earthen embankment. It was from behind this formidable fortification that our comrades-in-arms were finally able to halt the Yankee advance. By this time, our division had opened fire at the bluecoats to our front who had become observers of the dramatic scene unfolding to our left. I had gotten off three good rounds toward the battery to our front, when it seemed the sky caved in and I went to my knees, a crushing weight about my head and shoulders. The weight turned out to be the two hundred pounds of Captain McCarthy of the First Richmond Howitzers, McLaws's Artillery, who had seemingly run out of wind after his sprint from the station. Pointing this gray-coated trajectory toward Captain Carter, I heard him gasp out the reason for his unannounced visit: "Captain, I spotted two Napoleons parked down by the station doing nobody any good. My gunners are frazzled and none of them have the wind to move them forward, but if you could loan me a squad for that purpose, we could stop that Yankee formation on the left."

Well, as luck would have it, the loose-lipped Billy Richards chimed right in that our squad would be happy to oblige. It didn't seem that Captain Carter recognized this flagration of the chain of command since he immediately waved us off with Captain McCarthy, ordering us to return as soon as possible. Thus began my reluctant sprint back to the station and the mission which was to raise me one tick in the rank of sergeant. Nonetheless, I made sure Billy grabbed the tiller of one of the artillery pieces and his face was five shades redder by the time we got it up to the boxcar barricade where some ragged artillerists hobbled over to claim possession. Billy had little to say between labored gasps on the way back to the station where I allowed the boys a breather. To my recollection, he never volunteered for any duty for the rest of the war. There is nothing more strenuous for an infantryman than to be detached for a quick advance of the artillery. As we gathered ourselves for the sprint back to our trench, a glance toward McLaws's embattled division took in the good effects of our recent deliveries. The two Napoleons had commenced firing toward the Yankee divisions, which were now emerging from the line of woods west of town. We could see significant holes appearing in their ranks from our vantage point on the platform behind the station. There was no reply to these two requisitioned pieces since, as pointed out earlier, Hooker had chosen to place his entire complement of artillery among the smoldering linettes to our front. Once back in Texas, I remained convinced that the deployment of these two guns was responsible for the successful withdrawal of the First Corps to the other side of the Tennessee during the twilight hours of October 25, 1863. (Of course I never told Billy that!)

It had been our impression since arriving in the Valley of the Tennessee that nightfall came quickly as the autumn of the year progressed. This impression, however, was sorely contradicted during the desperate struggle we waged against Hooker's Army around Bridgeport, Alabama, during the late afternoon of October 25, 1863. The sun, partly obscured by the natural haze of Indian summer and the unnatural effluent from thirty thousand rifles, seemingly became stalled in its heavenly course. The entire scene became frozen in time like one of those mellowed tintypes I had viewed as a young enlistee back in Austin. Perhaps it was this connection that briefly turned my thoughts—harried now between receiving and relying shouted commands—to my parents and the last letter I had written them after the fight at the Brotherton Farm. Such thoughts, however, are but precursors to calamity in combat and I pushed them from my mind as we sought feverishly to disable the Yankee artillerists reloading their pieces to our front. Each man in the Texas Brigade knew that the life of the First Corps depended on protecting the bridgehead behind us until nightfall.

Thankfully, the Yankees had not yet directed any artillery fire at the bridge itself or at the locomotive shed obscured from view several hundred yards south of the station. In the final analysis, it was the sound of these steam engines being fired up rather than the view of any sunset that finally signaled us that the withdrawal across the Tennessee was about to begin.

McLaws's troops began a silent left-to-right withdrawal from behind their boxcar barricade about six P.M. that evening. The sheer bulk of those derailed monoliths did as much as the darkness in shielding this movement from the Yankees three hundred yards to their front whose confidence in the next day's assault blazed forth in newly-lit supper fires amidst the trees. With the ghost-like forms of McLaws's men still moving into and onto the waiting train behind us, the darkened locomotive broke into its first laborious pull for the Tennessee River Bridge. Immediately, shouts went up from the bluecoats to our front accentuated by the clang of artillery primers and tools against still-warm barrels. Now if it is true that experience is the best school, I had certainly learned one basic lesson during the term held between the Virginia Peninsula and Chickamauga Creek, i.e., the only tactic more confusing than a nighttime infantry attack is a nighttime artillery practice. This lesson, however, was exactly what made the evening action at Bridgeport Station the strangest gambit ever experienced by my fellow students in the Fourth Texas.

Although Hooker had placed the full complement of his artillery across the entire front of Jenkins's Division, only four pieces overlapped the now-critical space between the station and bridge four hundred yards to the south of our company. For this reason, Company B would be the last of the rearguard to leave Bridgeport. Yet if those four pieces were elevated to target the bridge or train pulling toward it, our entire corps would be trapped between the river and Hooker's overwhelming numbers. As we hurried off a pre-emptory volley in the direction of the cursing Yankee gunners, I too was tempted to curse the gamble that had wagered so much on the tenuous assumption that they would not target the bridge. Tempted, I say, because at that very moment my eyes beheld a ray of hope arching through the night sky before exploding above the two batteries nearest the river. Soon, amidst the rebel cheers and Yankee oaths, a second projectile preceded the delayed report of Captain McCarthy's other Napoleon placed over at the extreme right of the nearly-deserted boxcar barricade. Captain McCarthy and a small group of his Richmond Howitzers would be the only prize Howard's Germans would find in the morning.

A narrow slit-trench had been dug between the redan where the bulk of our division had been placed and the station now being cleared by the last boxcar full of McLaws's troops. When it became evident that the Yankees were intent on keeping the bridge intact, we persuaded Captain Carter to move over to the redan and exit via this trench toward the second train coming up from the engine house. As the last unit destined to leave Bridgeport, Company B would have to use its own natural steam to re-cross the bridge. Thankfully, the night was becoming more cloudy and a steady rain began to attend the silent withdrawal of the redan force toward the station, which, by this time, had begun to draw the fire of the enemy pieces to our front. It was through the flashes of these guns, however, that we were able to detect a solid line of crouching bluecoats moving out from behind the ruins toward the rapidly-emptying redan. Directing our fire to the left-oblique, we caved in the left flank of this line. In so doing, however, we called the attention of every bluecoat to the important role assigned our company. It was time for us to depart Bridgeport at the double-quick!

When the word finally came, I believe every man in the company set a personal best record for the quarter-mile dash back to the tracks. Despite their exhausted condition, Lieutenant Hays had all he could do to discourage some of the boys from continuing their sprint toward the departing cars carrying our division. Gratefully, despite the pouring rain, the six men in my squad seemed all too-ready to drop down behind the embankment as the Lieutenant ordered for the purpose of delivering one or two more volleys toward any bluecoat pursuers. With our wind thus restored, we turned our backs on Bridgeport Station and began our final run across the Tennessee River Bridge in the direction of our departing comrades.

About halfway across, we encountered several engineers laying a tarp over the railing of the catwalk to shelter the fuses being inserted into the barrels of black powder placed under the planking of the bridge. "You the last ones?" one called out as we passed. When Lieutenant Hays pointed out that Captain McCarthy's men were still continuing their work back at the boxcar barricade, the engineer officer replied, "They elected to leave by another route, Lieutenant. Have your men step lively now, we're about to set 'er off!" As we neared the east end of the bridge, the three engineers actually stampeded past our company as a thunderous roar reverberated up and over the Valley of the Tennessee. It seemed as if the breath of some unseen giant propelled me head-over-heels into the road from which we had embarked a mere ten days ago. Rolling to a painful stop, my backward glance encountered a disparate downpour of twisted iron and wood comingling with the October rains cascading into the river below.

We awoke in our sunken road bivouac the next morning much fatigued from our work of October 25th but uplifted in spirit by what had been accomplished. At noon we were formed up in the road as Old Pete galloped down the line with hat raised, stopping to congratulate each brigade commander. Each brigade in turn cheered Lee's "Old War Horse" when he had finished addressing its brigadier and so it went all the way over to McLaws's Division on the other side of the pike. The collective jist of all these congratulations was that our two divisions had invested and destroyed the major Federal supply base for the besieged Chattanooga garrison now commanded by Grant and Thomas. Furthermore, we had checkmated two corps from the Army of the Potomac on the opposite bank that would have been instrumental in attacking Bragg's left on Lookout Mountain. The news that this mission might occupy us for the rest of the winter was welcomed by the fact that the regiments left behind had done much to improve the comforts of our position.

Although numerous barrels of flour, salt pork, gunpowder and overcoats had been sent back to General Bragg, an adequate supply had been stored for our divisions in plank shelters built into the back side of the sunken road. In addition, the First Corps was now in possession of more tentage and canvas for shelter than it ever had in Virginia. With Colonel Alexander's artillery commanding the remnants of the Tennessee River Bridge, the bluecoats seemed content to assess the damage from their side. As November 1863 approached, we settled down as comfortable observers of Hooker's predicament while General Longstreet rode back to confer with General Bragg on Missionary Ridge.

As things turned out, we spent the rest of 1863 in our lines opposite Bridgeport. With the destruction of this supply center and the Tennessee River Bridge, Grant's immediate concerns became more mundane—feeding the Chattanooga garrison. To this end, instead of assuming offensive operations against the Army of Tennessee, Hooker's Army was assigned the task of rebuilding the rail line between Bridgeport and Stevenson, Alabama. At the same time, concerned that the single line from Nashville would be inadequate for supplying the several armies converging on Chattanooga, Grant stripped Sherman of a second division to help the one already assigned to Grenville Dodge for rebuilding the line between Nashville and Decatur, Alabama. To counter the immediate threat of starvation now looming over Thomas's Army of the Cumberland, Grant ordered Burnside to establish a new "cracker line" from Knoxville to Chattanooga. It seems Burnside had built up quite a supply of "Lincoln platforms" in the former place after being informed that General Longstreet had been detached from Bragg's siege line. Once this supply line had been established, Burnside himself was ordered to Chattanooga to take the place of the checkmated General Hooker.

The precious time that General Longstreet's alternative had purchased for General Bragg, however, would eventually come to naught if the latter could not be persuaded to assume the initiative against the now-separated and distracted Federals. By year's end, it became apparent to all that Bragg could not be so persuaded. It was almost as if our success in destroying the "cracker barrel" and isolating Hooker had confirmed his belief that the Federals would ultimately be forced to evacuate Chattanooga. On New Year's Day, 1864, General Longstreet held the last of his three conferences with

General Bragg since our investment of Bridgeport. With the latter's faith in "watching and waiting" still unshaken even as Burnside's men deployed on Williams Island, "Old Pete" played his last card, the "Fredericksburg card."

Urging Bragg to move off the narrow topographical crest of Missionary Ridge to the military crest below, he pointed out the wisdom of enveloping fields of fire reminiscent of his disposition of Pickett's and McLaws's Divisions below the Rappanhannock two winters ago. Bragg would listen to none of these alternatives, holding fast to his belief that the three redundant trench lines to his front would be sufficient since Grant was "obviously" preparing to attack his flanks on Lookout Mountain and Tunnel Hill. According to the grapevine telegraph, the last meeting between Generals Longstreet and Bragg ended with this admonition from the latter: "Your best service to this army, General Longstreet, will be to hasten an attack against General Burnside once you receive my signal that he has crossed over the river against us."

This signal from Bragg never came, for when the Federals finally attacked in late January 1864, it was his center that crumbled first to the previously chastised Army of the Cumberland. With this breakthrough, General Longstreet's strategy for bringing a "consolidated offensive" to the Tennessee Valley ended.

As we boarded the waiting trains for our circuitous return to Virginia, we heard that the "ugliest man in the Corps" had been ordered to Richmond as "personal military advisor" to President Davis. With Grant doing nothing to correct the North's delusion that he had ordered the all-out attack on Bragg's center, Lincoln promoted him to Commander-in-Chief of all Union Armies. Thus it was, that in the two additional months of Southern Independence purchased by "Old Pete's" alternative, only one capable AND honest general returned to Virginia. On this note, I conclude my final chapter in tribute to Miss Annie.

Val Giles
Sergeant, Company B
Fourth Texas Regiment

Seven

Alternatives after Appomattox ...

On April 9, 1865 at Appomattox Court House, Virginia, General Longstreet offered his last tactical alternative in the Civil War. "General," he said to the departing Lee, "unless he offers us honorable terms, come back and let us fight it out." As the Commander of Southern Armies rode off for his meeting with Ulysses Simpson Grant during that Palm Sunday truce, Old Pete characteristically and energetically prepared the remnants of the Army of Northern Virginia for the resumption of hostilities. As history records, the terms offered by General Grant were "honorable" and Longstreet, who had served as Grant's best man, was presumably one of those on whom they had a "happy effect." There was, however, a strained moment during Lee's absence that morning, which should be kept in mind if one is to evaluate the unique role that his "Old Warhorse" would play in the Reconstruction of the American Republic.

In the midst of Longstreet's final preparation for battle, a Union cavalry officer, with long blond hair streaming behind, charged through the Southern picket line and galloped up to proclaim in a brusque, excited voice, "I demand the unconditional surrender of this army." Recalling his reaction to this precipitous act years later, Longstreet would write,

> Custer was reminded that I was not the commander of the army, that he was within the lines of the enemy without authority, addressing a superior officer and in disrespect to General Grant as well as myself; that if I was the commander of the army, I would not receive the message. (Custer) became more moderate, saying it would be a pity to have more blood on the field and . . . satisfied, rode back to his command.[1]

Subsequently, Longstreet was one of three officers detailed by Lee to report to the McLean house in order to work out details of the surrender. As he rode between the two armies, the former recalled his last meeting with the Commander-in-Chief of the Armies of the United States. In 1858, four years after the bottle had separated Captain U. S. Grant from the army, he had approached Major Longstreet on a St. Louis street with five dollars, describing it as a debt payment from some forgotten card game played at the Jefferson Barracks. "Seeing the determination in the man's face," Longstreet recalled, "and in order to save him mortification, I took the money and shaking hands, we parted. The next time we met was at Appomattox." How Commander-in-Chief Grant would react to a reunion with the defeated head of the First Corps was soon to be answered.

> As I was passing through the room as one of the commissioners, General Grant looked up, recognized me, rose and with his old time cheerful greeting gave me his hand, and after passing a few remarks offered a cigar which was gratefully accepted.[2]

Thus, in these two contrasting meetings with Union officers on Palm Sunday 1865, Longstreet picked a median path that even Lee found difficult to discern in the fallen darkness of the Lost Cause. In his refusal to bend to the arrogance of his conquerors, "Old Pete" stood ready to resume pre-war friendships with Northerners of like mind. Longstreet, in short, was about to embark on a difficult bridge-building alternative that lay somewhere between his defeated comrades of "The Solid South" and those "Radical" Northerners who sought a political Appomattox by tirelessly "waving the bloody shirt" in its face well up to the end of the century.[3]

Back at the war's "turning point" on Gettysburg's Seminary Ridge, the young scholar-soldier Jeremiah Gere thought he divined a remedy if the Radical Republicans succeeded in destroying America's two-party system as a result of military victory. Southerners, he "reckoned," would just have to work through the Republican Party. Yet James Longstreet's political bridgebuilding would require more than one piling, for it would be aimed at preserving bipartisanship for the next generation of Americans. To Mrs. Longstreet, this bipartisan bridge-building campaign was the toughest her husband ever fought. "Old comrades," he would lament to her, "passed me on the street without speaking." Initially, the most obvious reasons for this rejection by the "un-reconstructed rebels" were twofold: 1) Ex–Lieutenant General James Longstreet was the first high-ranking Confederate officer to publicly counsel both submission to the Reconstruction Acts AND support for the Republican Party. 2) Longstreet's was the first amnesty granted to a former officer of the United States who had joined the rebellion and number two looked mightily like a reward for number one!

If this analysis had been an analysis of the causes/effects of events rather than the causes/effects of one individual's alternative choices, much could be written about the seismic events of this century that caused a Republican from Longstreet's home state of Georgia to be installed as Speaker of the House one hundred and thirty years after Appomattox. In addition, much of the same type of analysis could be applied to understanding how Republicans from Mississippi and Texas ascended into the influential posts of Senate and House Majority Leaders at the same time. Yet, given the fact that such has not been our focus, one would still search in vain for a more significant individual than James Longstreet in preserving a two-party alternative for the defeated South and the consequent avoidance of a "political Appomattox" for the nation as a whole somewhere down the line.

Not Abraham Lincoln who was assassinated by a "southern sympathizer" five days after Appomattox or Andrew Johnson, a "southern sympathizer" politically assassinated by the Radical Republicans three years later; certainly not the unrepentant Davis or the aloof Lee or Grant for that matter. Throw in the social reformers like General Oliver Howard, Booker T. Washington, and Lauren Towne and elevation of the freedmen to citizenship becomes their singular focus of Reconstruction. In short, no individual from the last century has as much to teach America today about the need to preserve its delicate two-party balance amidst the hue and cry of conflicting interest groups than "Old Pete." In a time and place where the public agenda was increasingly being written by night riders, lynch law, carpetbag fraud, and bribery in high places, it took patience to seek out common ground and uncommon courage to fashion a bridge between conflicting interest groups.

As he had done so often on the battlefield, Longstreet early sought Lee's endorsement of his alternatives before committing to battle. Lee, however, declined to endorse his "Old Warhorse's" campaign of preserving a bipartisan alternative in the postwar South, replying in the last letter to pass between the two,

> I have avoided all discussion of political questions since the cessation of hostilities. And have in my own conduct and in my recommendation to others endeavored to conform to existing circumstances. I consider this the part of wisdom as well as of duty. But while I think we should act under the law . . . imposed upon us, I cannot think the course pursued by the dominant political party the best for the interests of the country, and therefore cannot . . . give them any approval.[4]

On March 4, 1869, Lieutenant General U. S. Grant was inaugurated President of the United States and submitted his best man's name to the Senate for confirmation as United States Surveyor of Customs at New Orleans. This appointment proved to be the first litmus test of Longstreet's commitment to postwar bipartisanship since this $6,000-a-year appointment created as much outcry in the North as in the South over his acceptance of it. Particularly vociferous in their opposition were those Pennsylvania senators who had not forgotten the invasion of their state by the Army of Northern Virginia on its way to Gettysburg in 1863. Because of such bitter denunciations, Longstreet even considered refusing his first national appointment because he did not wish to "compromise or reflect upon a too-affectionate kindness of his kinsman and late antagonist, the President of the United States."

In the end, however, Longstreet's desire to bridge the

bitter gulf separating Radical Republicans and un-reconstructed rebels caused him to assume a position that placed him in the middle of one of the bloodiest confrontations of the postwar years. In accepting Grant's appointment, a dual role awaited him when he reached New Orleans—one federal and one state. Louisiana Governor Henry Warmoth, a former Federal officer sympathetic with the Radicals, saw fit to appoint his old adversary Adjutant-General of the State Militia upon his arrival in the Crescent City. Old Pete proceeded to make this militia, however, into a visible, overt symbol of his post-War bridge-building campaign. Although called out frequently to enforce obedience to court orders and discourage riots against the established government, the faces of this militia were those of 2,500 ex-Confederate veterans and 2,500 Black Freedmen. Yet the chaotic mix that festered at the mouth of the Father of Waters after the Civil War revealed little common ground upon which to build a consensus of any kind. As Burger and Betterworth note in their *South of Appomattox,*

> For eight years the blunt, honest soldier was caught in the swarm of unscrupulous swindlers, opportunists, political adventurers of both races, all party stripes and all degrees of honesty and dishonesty.
>
> In Louisiana there was even from the first, a fierce contest for power not only between Democrats and Republicans but between rival factions in each of the major parties. In some elections, as many as five different sets of candidates of various splinter groups were on the ballot. At times, there were also several sets of election commissioners, each determined to certify the results differently. Several candidates would then be declared elected for the same office. Rival legislatures met at the same time, each declaring itself the legal one.

Once, when Congress formed a committee to investigate the root causes of the chaos in New Orleans, one Radical Republican eagerly fired off this question at the Federal Army Commander for the city: "Which side did General Longstreet represent?" The answer was a simple testimony to the search for common ground, i.e., "I cannot say that he represented either." Finally, on September 14, 1874, the factional discord in the Crescent City erupted into one of the bloodiest, single pitched battles of the Reconstruction Period. Angered over Washington's imposition of a corrupt carpetbag government under Governor W. P. Kellogg, whereby both the state debt and tax levies had quadrupled over eight years, armed White Leaguers violently engaged the New Orleans police who had been dispatched to disarm them.

Three to five thousand armed citizens poured into the vicinity of Canal Street calling for the forcible ouster of carpetbag/freedman rule throughout the entire State of Louisiana. As a smaller band of uniformed police and militiamen moved down the street to confront this unruly mob, a lone horseman rode out from their midst and took up a position in the space separating the two factions. Adjutant-General Longstreet, hat in hand as so many of his veterans had remembered him, urged the now-silent crowd to disperse, return to their homes, and place their faith in the power of the ballot. Rising up from the crowd in defiant reply came the rebel yell, which had punctuated the ears of the South's enemies from Manassas to Chickamauga and one observer swore later that Lee's "Old Warhorse" was visibly moved. Still, Longstreet sat his horse between the increasingly hostile forces moving toward him. Suddenly, the first shots rang out, hitting the Adjutant General of Louisiana. With blood ushering from several wounds, "Old Pete" turned mechanically yet resignedly to the preparation of his outnumbered force for battle.

Eventually, the Federal Army was called in to restore order that day since the White Leaguers had a base of support that stretched far beyond Louisiana to encompass all the states of the former Confederacy. Longstreet's stand during the clash in New Orleans, however, took on a symbolic significance that cut the ground out from under the Radical Republican argument that there was no hope of reconciliation with former Confederates—that self-same rationale for "Waving the Bloody Shirt" at election time. A young reporter from the *New Orleans Picayune* who rushed to interview the recuperating general several days after his stand on Canal Street was unable to uncover any evidence of recrimination for the events of September 14th.

> <u>Reporter:</u> I myself have heard men say that they would "shoot Longstreet on sight." General, these people seem to be pretty savage on you down here, don't they?
> <u>Longstreet:</u> I don't know. Maybe they do.
> <u>Reporter:</u> Why yes, they call you a recreant, a traitor and they say you've betrayed the interests of the South.
> <u>Longstreet:</u> There exists a difference of opinion as to what the interests of the South are. I think they are one thing, and they think they are another. That's the way we happened to get separated.

(The young reporter apparently left this interview with a less-sensational story for his editor, but a much more valuable lesson in personal and political moderation.)

At the nation's Centennial in 1876, the conflicting interests unleashed during Radical Reconstruction were reflected in the presidential election returns. A special bipartisan electoral commission was formed by Congress to devise a compromise solution to the double sets of returns received by the electoral college for Rutherford B. Hayes, Republican, and Samuel J. Tilden, Democrat. During the trying days when the special commission labored to find a bipartisan solution to this unique problem, President Grant received a note from his former best man, now the spokesman for "the Republican Party, South." Apparently the election returns in Louisiana had shown that many White Leaguers had heeded his request to place their faith in the ballot box and had chosen the Democratic slate over that of the Republican slate headed by the freedman, S. B. Packard. Longstreet strongly urged the president to refrain from using any federal intervention to install the Republican slate. Such intervention, Longstreet wrote, would not only reverse the will of the Louisiana majority in 1876, but

> . . . it will be better for the Republican Party, South, if this idea can be adopted. For if the Packard government is forced upon this state, the greater part, if not all of the Southern men who have been identified with the Republican Party in the hope that some day the party might be put upon a basis that might justify their efforts, in giving it PERMANENT ORGANIZATION, will be obliged to abandon their hopes.[5]

Grant acquiesced in this recommendation and when Rutherford B. Hayes was awarded the presidency through the Compromise of 1877, it was conditioned on his promise to end military occupation of the former Confederate states. As Longstreet watched the last bluecoat march out of the Crescent City, the new Republican president sat down in Washington to write the first of three federal appointments, Deputy Collector of Internal Revenue for the United States. Following were appointments as Minister to Turkey and finally as United States Marshal for his home state of Georgia, a post he held until 1884. A *New York Times* reporter, known for his dispassionate articles dealing with the politics of the "Brown Decades," observed in 1882,

> There is an element in the Republican Party . . . that may turn up as an important factor. (It) centers on General Longstreet, who is now United States Marshal in Georgia. General Longstreet has been a consistent Republican since the war, and since has been working effectively in Washington through Senator Mahone whose division was in Longstreet's Corps in the late war. Longstreet is trustworthy, popular and strong and seems to have arranged very satisfactorily . . . for the encouragement of Independent movement.[6]

Now reciprocal recognition of Old Pete's campaign to build a bipartisan alternative for the defeated South rested with his former comrades-in-arms. His efforts had been commended by Washington and the Northern press, but he still carried the physical and emotional wounds inflicted by the White Leaguers in New Orleans. Bipartisan bridge-building still needed *two* pylons.

On May 1, 1886, largely at Mrs. Longstreet's urging, he made a courageous attempt to heal the rift with his former comrades at a large gathering in Atlanta. Jefferson Davis was to unveil a monument to the late Senator Ben H. Hill, with the governor of Georgia and other high-ranking Confederates on the dias. During the ceremony, the large crowd (including 50,000 Confederate veterans) already at a high pitch of enthusiasm over the introduc-

tion of its former president, grew even more excited at the
sight of a large mounted figure approaching the platform
clothed in the gray uniform of a Lieutenant-General in
the Confederate Army. It was Longstreet, who had come
uninvited to show that much of his heart still lay with the
Lost Cause. The crowd grew quiet as Old Pete mounted
the steps and moved toward the only president the Confederacy had known. An observer described what happened next.

> When General Longstreet was within about ten feet of the
> canopy where Mr. Davis sat, the old gentleman arose and
> hastened to meet the General. When the two came to-
> gether, Mr. Davis threw his arms around General Long-
> street's neck and the two leaders embraced with great
> emotion. The meaning of the reconciliation was clear and
> instantly had a profound effect on the Confederate veter-
> ans who saw it. With a great shout, they showed their
> joy.[7]

From that moment on, with but few exceptions,
Longstreet was again recognized as Lee's "Old Warhorse." At a parade of the Society of the Army of Northern
Virginia in Richmond, marching veterans streamed out
of ranks to greet him as he sat in his carriage on the side-
lines. "They shook my hand until they made my arm
ache," he wrote. "At another time I was seized by a crowd
of old soldiers and wrapped up completely in Confederate
flags." Such treatment was even more remarkable in
light of Longstreet's established habit of attending Grand
Army of the Republic (GAR) meetings where he was frequently invited to be the keynote speaker. At such times,
he rarely failed to reminisce about their former commander, U. S. Grant, as "my lifetime personal friend,
kindest when I was most fiercely assaulted."

As indicated in the introduction, the fiercest assault of the war years had occurred at Gettysburg where a record number of Americans had given their "last full measure of devotion." A case could be made that within that three-day contest, the bloodiest assault occurred in the Peach Orchard on July 2, 1863 when Longstreet's divisions reduced the salient pushed forward by Union General Sickles, who lost his leg in the charge. This loss is what makes Sickles's reminiscence of St. Patrick's Day 1892 in Atlanta such a poignant testimony to Longstreet's role in furthering Abraham Lincoln's hope for the nation expressed in his Second Inaugural Address—"to bind up the Nation's wounds." Although the rebel yell had greeted Sickles and Longstreet as they came into the banquet hall arm-in-arm, it was Longstreet who started the evening's festivities in leading the assemblage in singing, "The Star Spangled Banner." Sickles described the end of the evening thusly:

We decided to go to our lodgings long before the end of the revel, which appeared likely to last until daybreak. When we descended to the street, we were unable to find a carriage, but Longstreet proposed to be my guide; and though the streets were dark and the walk a long one, we reached my hotel in fairly good form. Not wishing to be outdone on courtesy, I said—"Longstreet, the streets of Atlanta are very dark and it is very late, and you are somewhat deaf and rather infirm; now I must escort you to your headquarters."

"All right," said Longstreet, "come on . . . "

When we arrived at his stopping place and were about to separate, as I supposed, he turned to me and said—"Sickles, the streets of Atlanta are very dark and you are lame, and a stranger here and do not know the way back to your hotel; I must escort you home."

"Come along, Longstreet," was my answer. On our way to the hotel, I said to him—"Old fellow, I hope you are sorry for shooting off my leg at Gettysburg. I suppose I will have to forgive you for it some day."

"Forgive me?" Longstreet exclaimed. "You ought to thank me for leaving you one good leg to stand on, after the mean way you behaved to me at Gettysburg!"

How often we performed escort duty for each other on that eventful night I have never been able to recall with precision; but I am quite sure that I shall never forget St. Patrick's Day in 1892 at Atlanta, Georgia, when Longstreet and I enjoyed the good banquet of the Knights of St. Patrick.[8]

The recollection above takes on greater significance when one realizes that Major General Daniel Sickles was no starry-eyed nineteenth-century Romantic or converted Bible-thumper. He had been indicted for murder after killing a man in a duel over an "affair of honor." Northern political connections had secured his reprieve and appointment to a commission and when the war was over, he harbored sufficient resentment against the Confederacy for the Radical Republicans to appoint him military governor over the state where hopes of Southern Independence had begun—South Carolina. After being called a "conceited cuckold" by Andrew Johnson for abolishing South Carolina's "Black Codes," he had "stumped" up to Washington to pressure wavering senators to vote guilty in the impeachment trial of a president whom he considered too soft on the defeated South. This campaign having failed by one vote, Sickles dropped off his amputated leg at the Smithsonian Institution to keep the memory of his personal sacrifice for the Union alive for future generations.

To the end of his life in 1904, the twin lightning rods

of Longstreet's life remained his role at Gettysburg and his campaign for bipartisanship in the postwar South. Denounced bitterly for the former by fellow-officers like Jubal Early and Lee's artillery chief, Pendleton, it is important to note that these attacks began only after Longstreet committed himself to the latter. Meanwhile, Robert E. Lee had gone to his grave claiming, "It took a dozen blunders to lose Gettysburg, and I committed a good many of them." Finally, the telling delineation between the motives and methods used by "Old Pete's" critics came in 1875 when Lee's Chief of Staff, Colonel Walter H. Taylor, wrote Longstreet: "I regard it as a great mistake on the part of those who, perhaps because of political differences, now undertake to criticize and attack your war record."

At the dedication of Grant's Tomb in 1897, Longstreet was invited to be the guest of honor by Vice President Adlai E. Stevenson. The *New York Times* did a credible job of describing the occasion as one of national reconciliation. The *New York Tribune,* not to be outdone, detailed one of its reporters to follow the old general home for a more personal story. This correspondent almost missed his quarry (but not quite)—

I had looked for a large, old-fashioned Southern place, with pillars and a wide hall. Instead, the house was an ordinary story-and-half farmhouse, such as a Northern carpenter might build. A board nailed to a tree offered wine for sale at a very low price, and I saw an extensive vineyard across the road . . . there I came upon him, scissors in hand, busily pruning his vines. He is a big old man, stooping a little now, and slow of gait. His hair is as white as wool, but his skin is ruddy as though sleep and good digestion were still his to command. We talked for a time about his garden and vineyard.

"I get out every afternoon!" he said, "and work about. I find the sun and air do me good."

One of his arms is a little disabled, and he is quite deaf in one ear. He could not hear very well in the open air, and at his suggestion we returned to the house.

"I live with my tenant. He is a veteran of The Northern Army," he said at the door and there was a slight smile about his eyes.[9]

Of course, some unreconstructed rebels would never forgive Longstreet for his post-Appomattox blueprint for repairing the "House Divided." The United Confederate Veterans at Wilmington, North Carolina, declined to express regret at his passing on January 2, 1904 while the Daughters of the Confederacy voted against sending any flowers to his funeral.

Shortly before his death, Longstreet had mused, "I hope to live long enough to see my surviving comrades march side by side with the Union veterans along Pennsylvania Avenue, and then I can die happy." I have not uncovered any evidence that Longstreet ever viewed such a parade, but at this point, I would more than welcome any evidence to the contrary. Certainly, at gatherings in Atlanta and New York, he came very close to its realization—more close it appears to me than any of his contemporaries. His last alternative campaign for the South had succeeded in freeing it from the stultifying conviction that there would never be another cause except the one that had been "Lost."

In wrapping itself in "The Conquered Banner," the "Solid South" had blinded itself to what both its Founding Fathers (like Madison) and Favorite Sons (like Calhoun) had shown it from *Federalist #10* to the South Carolina Exposition & Protest—that bipartisan debate marks the only safe road in America between the Tyranny of a Centralized Government on one hand and the Anarchy of hooded night-riders on the other. To this extent, one is prone to agree with Mrs. Longstreet that her husband's last campaign alternative was also his most difficult. Today, poised at the bridgehead of a new millennium, a much-divided America would do well to pause and reconsider the alternatives that come from "Listening to Old Pete."

. . . and an Afterword

Today, "as in Lincoln's time," writes Mark Gerzon in *A House Divided,*

> a struggle is being waged for America's soul. Just as the issue of slavery was fundamental to the destiny of our country, so are the scores of issues that divide us today. But now we are not divided into two armies wearing blue and gray uniforms and fighting over slavery. Rather we are fragmented by conflicting belief systems which turn almost any issue into flash points for bitterness, anger, hatred and other violence. The range and intensity of these disputes has become almost overwhelming . . . almost NO CAUSE COMMANDS CONSENSUS.[10]

If "no cause commands consensus," is our nation's motto "E Pluribus Unum" irrelevant today? More importantly, what has happened to its underpinning, the art of bipartisan compromise, which Longstreet and others sought to resuscitate after Appomattox? There are, of course, two components to this last question. One component simply implies that the multiplicity of issues assailing our national consciousness has made bipartisanship

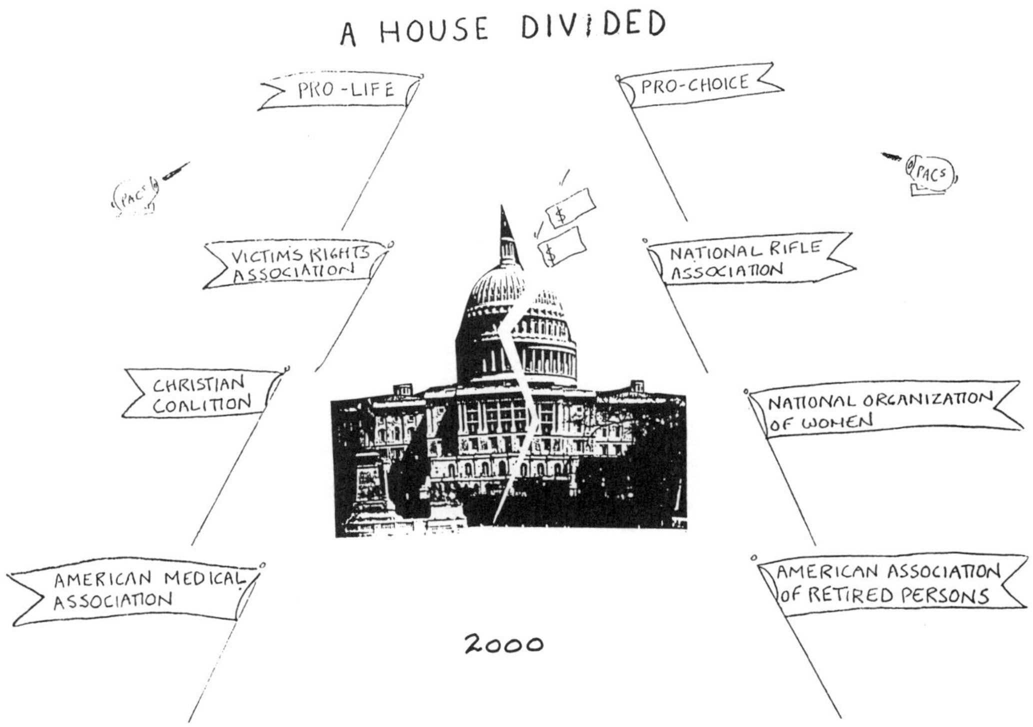
A HOUSE DIVIDED
PRO-LIFE
PRO-CHOICE
PACS
PACS
$
$
VICTIMS RIGHTS ASSOCIATION
NATIONAL RIFLE ASSOCIATION
CHRISTIAN COALITION
NATIONAL ORGANIZATION OF WOMEN
AMERICAN MEDICAL ASSOCIATION
AMERICAN ASSOCIATION OF RETIRED PERSONS
2000

more difficult, if not impossible. On December 29, 1997, for example, the mayor of our nation's largest city suggested through the National Broadcasting Corporation that the abolition of party "labels" would be a productive first step in addressing the complexities rising from the rapid urbanization of our country, i.e., just let people vote for the best candidate without reference to "Republican" or "Democrat."

The second component of the above question deals with the "art of compromise"—the ability to listen to one's opponent with the object of finding a common meeting ground. This component goes far deeper than the political realm and into the more nebulous field of social psychology. Irrespective of what is happening to the agendas of the Republican and Democratic parties, America's citizens have seemingly jettisoned common civility from their public discourse. Individual Americans, for whatever reason, no longer subscribe to the basic tenet of democratic discourse i.e.— "I may disagree with what you say, but will defend to the death your right to say it." Meanwhile, the connecting ribbons of our Republic from Washington, D.C. to the interior are filled with the "road rage" of those who have surrendered to the onslaught of incivility in their personal and public lives. Once having arrived at our respective destinations,

> . . . we hear divisive, destructive charges and counter-charges all too often about trivia. The media, the courts, the political campaigns—all have become gladiator's arenas. Trust between citizens have been replaced by fear and the more Americans fear each other, the weaker we become. At a point in history when no nation on earth is powerful enough to defeat us, we may defeat ourselves.[11]

On May 27, 1998, the non-partisan Council on Civil Society published an independent and updated confirmation of Mr. Gerzon's thesis in "A Call to Civil Society." Chaired by Jean Elshtain of the University of Chicago, the Council's members included United States Senators Dan Coats (R-IN) and Joseph Lieberman (D-CT) as well as public opinion analyst Daniel Yankelovich and academics like Francis Fukuyama. Concurring with some of the same trends noted by Gerzon above, the "Call to Civil Society" laments that the loss of a public civility creates a lack of "confidence that we as Americans are United by shared values."[12] Providing specific examples of the spread of uncivil behavior in the 1990s, the report cites baseball star Roberto Alomar spitting in the face of an American League umpire, Madonna proclaiming her need for (and giving birth to) a baby sans marriage, and President Clinton's consultant Dick Morris parlaying a prostitution scandal into a lucrative book contract.[13]

Today, Mark Gerzon and other contemporary observers of our "House Divided" believe America's salvation lies in a "new patriotism." The New Patriot is actuated by a primary desire to build bridges between conflicting belief systems and has no "special interest" other than finding common ground upon which more and more Americans can stand together, i.e.—UNITED. After reviewing the various characteristics that mark this "New Patriot," I saw many that were illustrative of Longstreet's post-Appomattox alternative. Let us examine five of these characteristics in light of that alternative to support my contention that "Old Pete" may have been one of the first "New Patriots" who set out to repair "A House Divided."

1. Take Stock before Taking Sides—The first characteristic of the "New Patriot" is to think and act independ-

ently of the partisan "bully"— i.e. "You're either WITH US or AGAINST US."

*As the highest-ranking ex–Confederate officer to embrace the Republican Party after Appomattox, James Longstreet epitomized this trait more than any of his contemporaries. In such a role, he probably acted more independently of the "partisan bully" more than any other figure in the postwar era, sustaining the bullets of blue-coat and white leaguer alike with "malice toward none" as far as the historic record shows. Assailed equally by Radical Republicans and un-reconstructed rebels, his "independent movement" showed both that the majority of Americans were neither as vindictive as Thaddeus Stevens or as noble as a "Marse Robert." In this respect, he went further than Johnson or Grant, Lee or George Washington Carver to "bind up the Nation's wounds," as Lincoln had envisioned in his second inaugural address.

2. Think like a Minority, because You are One—"Today," Gerzon writes the New Patriot realizes that "no ethnic group is the mainstream, no group is a standard for Americanness." He/she is cognizant of the fact that the 1990 census identified 300 races, 600 Indian tribes, 70 Hispanic groups, and 75 multiracial combinations.

*Eighty years before President Harry Truman ordered the integration of the Armed Forces of the United States, Longstreet, as Adjutant-General of the Louisiana militia, organized and led the first biracial peacekeeping force in the United States. Comprised of equal parts ex–Confederate veterans and black freedman, this was the force that Longstreet halted near Canal Street in New Orleans before riding out alone to reason with and take the first bullet from the White Leaguers on September 14, 1874. In this respect, Longstreet accomplished after our most-divisive conflict what Lincoln, Frederick

Douglass, and Robert Gould Shaw could not do during the struggle for "Liberty and Union"—the formation of a fully-integrated military force dedicated to preserving the Republican form of government guaranteed to the states under the Constitution.

3. Avoid Exaggeration, Hyperbole, and other Rhetorical Excess—Mr. Gerezon's example for the New Patriot here is taken from Lincoln's advice to the first Republican Convention in Illinois: "Let us appeal to the sense of patriotism of the people and not to their prejudices."

*From his reasoned response to Custer's arrogance at Appomattox to his appeal for the armed White Leaguers to choose "ballots over bullets," Longstreet spoke in reasoned terms of commonality, eschewing an all-too-easy resort to the bombast of "spread eagle oratory." One searches his letters, interviews, and speeches in vain for the overblown rhetoric so characteristic of the public (and private) men of his generation. Even when a young reporter from the *New Orleans Picayune* pointed out that his enemies "would shoot Longstreet on sight" as a "recreant and traitor," Old Pete assessed the hostile rhetoric as "a difference of opinion as to what the interests of the South are." I THINK they are one thing," said Lee's Old Warhorse and "they THINK they are another. That's the way we happened to get SEPARATED." Against the contentious backdrop of the "Stormy Sixties," Longstreet's relations with Grant and Davis, Freedman and unreconstructed rebel reflected an awareness of what former Senator Bill Bradley warns us of today—

Spinning out racist clichés and stereotypes, scurrilous character attacks and zingy one-liners is not the talk of a vibrant civil society. They are the yelps of demagogues.

4. Practice Humility—The fourth characteristic of the New Patriot, who Gerzon believes must be America's bridge-builder in the New Millennium, is humility. Humility in this sense is a reasoned acceptance that one can NOT speak for ALL or lay monopolistic claim on the TRUTH or even what is RIGHT in EVERY SITUATION. Reflective of this characteristic was the observation by Carl Jung, whom the author of *A House Divided* calls "one of the wisest students of the human mind."

> I do not forget that my voice is but one voice, my experience a mere drop in the sea, my knowledge no greater than the visual field in a microscope, my eye a mirror reflecting a small corner of the world.

*As far back as October 10, 1863 when the president of the Confederacy had given Longstreet a golden opportunity to lead the popular chorus denouncing Braxton Bragg's perceived incompetence, he demurred. The alternative he chose up on Missionary Ridge that day was a military tactic designed to resurrect Southern chances for Independence rather than a political one to advance himself into the command of the Army of Tennessee. As he noted shortly before his death, "I am not prompted by any desire to do or to attempt to do great things. I only wish to do what I regard as my duty." We latter-day citizens of "A House Divided" might well ask ourselves, "when was the last time I heard that assessment from a public figure?"

5. Seek Goals Greater than Victory. This is the fifth characteristic of the New Patriotism that Gerzon feels critical to the revitalization of our motto, "E Pluribus Unum." The search for common ground amidst a myriad of conflicting special interest groups precludes getting

ONE'S own way. Overcoming one's individual ego for the sake of the common good, however, is more difficult today than at any other time in our history. As indicated in the prologue above, the Natural Rights of Jefferson's eighteenth century has leached downward through State's Rights of the last century to engulf us with the highly individualistic rights of the "ME GENERATION." The result of such a leaching is that many today confuse "doing one's own thing" as a natural evolution of a personal War for Independence. Yet if our Zeitgeist at the bridge to the New Millennium is to assert oneself over the "other guy," the other guy will soon give back to one as good as he gets and social conflict becomes self-perpetuating. Nowhere is this tendency more evident than in the rising tide of lawsuits and counter-lawsuits that are engulfing the courtrooms of "A House Divided." As former presidential candidate George McGovern notes,

America is in the midst of a new civil war, a war that threatens to undercut the civil basis of our society. The weapons of choice are not bullets and bayonets, but abusive lawsuits brought by an army of trial lawyers subverting our system of civil justice while enriching themselves.[14]

*Mrs. Longstreet knew more intimately than anyone the personal sacrifices her husband had made in preserving bipartisan alternatives in a country devastated by civil war. "To me," she said,

he has always been a figure of more sublime courage in the . . . years that followed than on any of the brilliant fields of the Civil War. And I love best to think of him, not as the warrior leading his legions to victory, but as the grand citizen after the war was ended, nobly dedicating

himself to the rehabilitation of his broken people, offering
a brave man's homage to flag of the established government, and standing steadfast in all the passions, prejudices and persecutions of that unhappy period.[15]

The "Father of the Constitution," James Madison,
described FACTIONS as the greatest threat to our Constitutional form of government. "By a FACTION," the
Virginian wrote in *Federalist Ten,* "I understand a
number of citizens, whether amounting to a majority or a
minority of the whole, who are united and actuated by
some common impulse or INTEREST ADVERSE to the
Rights of other citizens or the PERMANENT . . .
AGGREGATE interests of the COMMUNITY."

To date, the American Civil War represents the ultimate factional conflict. I have chosen but one figure who
played a central role in this conflict and its aftermath in
hopes that a "factionalized" readership could appreciate
the possibilities of alternative conflict resolution when
backed by tact and individual courage. As stated above,
today's special interest groups (only partly-pictured
above) are more numerous and destructive of American
UNITY than those envisioned by Madison or Abraham
Lincoln. It is no longer so simple as North versus South.
Many of us belong to several of Gerzon's "divided states"
at the same time and the absence of infantry, cavalry, and
artillery does little to mitigate the danger to our national
identity.

Today, even Madison's remedy for the dangers of faction seem obsolete—a Republican form of government
based on "indirect representation." Certainly he believed
a government comprised of representatives of New Eng-
land shipbuilders, Virginia tobacco planters and Pitts-
burgh iron mongers could do little else but seek common

ground. The "passions of the people" were thus filtered through the art of compromise, while at the same time a tyranny of such diverse representation at the center was practically impossible—except as viewed by Madison's fellow Southerners in 1860! No doubt Longstreet's campaign to restore bipartisan debate after the Civil War can provide inspiration for Gerzon's "New Patriotism." Now, however, special interest groups have pushed past partisan distinctions and entered the halls of Congress itself as per the illustration above. One specific example of this can serve for many. (*Unum servis Pluribus?*)

During the first Congressional election campaign of 1998, special interest groups displaced both the Republican and Democratic candidates in "getting out the message" to citizens of California's central coast. In a trend that has been accelerating since 1994—and which is expected to increase in key congressional races next year—national special interest groups with "deep pockets" flooded this district's air waves and newspapers with such a large volume of graphic advertisements that it became practically impossible for Republican Tom Bordonaro and Democrat Lois Capps to be heard by the electorate.[16]

Unlike the candidates, special interest groups are free to raise and spend unlimited sums of money in political campaigns thanks to a loophole in campaign finance laws opened up by recent Supreme Court rulings, i.e. as long as such groups remain "independent" of the candidates and do not "synchronize" their campaigns with those candidates, their efforts are protected by Free Speech guarantees of the first Amendment.[17] Republican Bordonaro, who planned to base his campaign on the issues of education and health care, for instance, turned on NBC-TV one morning this past spring to find that the

Campaign for Working Families was supporting him for taking a position against late-term abortion. Not to be outdone, the National Abortion Rights Action League purchased airtime to denounce the affiliation of the Campaign for Working Families with religious rightist, Gary Bauer, leaving some Californians with the mistaken impression that Bauer, a non-Californian, was a candidate for something. Although this latter advertisement was supportive of the position on abortion taken by Democrat Capps, her name was never mentioned. Capps, who was campaigning to fill the vacant seat left by the death of her husband, later switched on the television to encounter a spot purchased by a group called Americans for Limited Terms, asking voters to "personally thank" her for signing a pledge not to serve more than three terms in Congress. On Tuesday, March 3, 1998, Democrat Capps won the special election to which she, along with her Republican opponent, Bordonaro, feel they were just "spectators."

When the day arrives wherein our representatives become mere "spectators" of million-dollar media blitzes waged by special interest groups, the Republican remedy for limiting factional discord envisioned by Madison will be destroyed as well as the possibilities of bipartisan compromise for which Longstreet campaigned after America's bloodiest factional conflict. "The situation is out of control," said Washington political analyst, Stuart Rothenberg, viewing the California campaign. "These groups are taking the campaigns away from the candidates . . . the inmates are taking over the asylum." Capp's supporters, who showed up to share in the fruits of her victory in the first Congressional contest of 1998, were instead sobered by her lament:

This situation is endangering democracy. These groups

don't pay any attention to the candidates. What's so arrogant is that they're not interested in the people of any local district. They only want to push their one issue and . . . then we wonder why so many people don't vote. It's bad for all of us.[18]

Back on Seminary Ridge in 1863, Jere Gere lamented that the election of 1860 did not reflect the majority will of the people who had voted for someone other than Abraham Lincoln. Certainly the vagaries of the electoral college that he targeted have long since been noted in the media and the halls of academia and are hence "beyond our poor power to add or detract" in these closing comments. Today, the greatest threat to our government "of the people, by the people and for the people" comes from the pervasive influence of special interest groups. Any campaign finance reform not directed at loosening their balkanizing grasp on our representative form of government will fail to repair our "House Divided." Although Senator Thompson's (R-TN) Committee on Campaign Finance Reform "started out as a partisan committee and ended a partisan committee," both Senator John McCain (R-AZ) and Russel Feingold (D-WI) were buoyed by the hope contained in that time-worn adage, "As Maine goes, so goes the nation."

Acting through an initiative, the people of Maine provide full public financing for those candidates who refuse to raise or accept private monies. This procedure alone could "revolutionize" politics notes *The Washington Post*.[19] Joining this innovation with the president's suggestion that the Federal Communications Commission offer political candidates free broadcast time, would go far to break the grip of private-interest monies on our electioneering process. Further, if the War between the

States was predicated on a "state's right" to *nullify* the laws and actions of the federal government, certainly the role of state primaries as a determinant of the federal executive must be replaced. The concept of national primaries would go far to break the unreasonable influence of those few states like New Hampshire and Iowa whose early primaries give an unfair push to that individual seeking the presidency of two-hundred and fifty million people. This reform, of course, would threaten those quadrennial bashes known as "party conventions," but the American people would have a more representative horn to blow than those few politicos sporting select passes and funny hats who act up before television cameras at some Miami Beach convention center.

After being bloodied and ostracized for his bipartisan stand during the Reconstruction of our Nation, "Old Pete" showed in his note to President Grant that he could still distinguish between political right and might in the election returns of America's centennial year. As the first of the "New Patriots," his historic alternatives to entrenched power and selfish interests serve as an inspiring example to those who would "bind up the Nation's wounds."

Notes

Chapter One

1. J. Persico, *My Enemy My Brother* (MacMillian Company, New York, 1962), p. 187.
2. D. S. Freeman, *Lee's Lieutenants* (Charles Scribner's Sons, New York, 1944), p. 144.
3. Williams, Current, Freidel, *U.S. History to 1876* (Knopf, New York, 1959), p. 1.
4. James Longstreet, *From Manassas to Appomattox* (Mallard Press, New York, 1941), p. 144.
5. Ibid.
6. Freeman, op. cit., pp. 107–108.
7. Longstreet, op. cit., p. 357.
8. Freeman, op. cit., pp. 120–121.
9. S. E. Morrison & H. Commager, *Growth of the American Republic* (Oxford University Press, New York, 1962), p. 765.
10. Freeman, op. cit.
11. Freeman, op. cit., pp. 144–145.

Chapter Two

1. J. Persico, *My Enemy My Brother* (MacMillan Company, New York, 1962), pp. 214–216.
2. Ibid.
3. Ibid., p. 13.
4. Ibid., p. 14.
5. J. F. Cooper in *The American Tradition in Literature* (W. W. Norton and Co., New York, 1962), pp. 406–431.
6. Ibid.
7. Persico, op. cit.

Chapter Three

1. Mary Laswell, *Rags and Hope* (Coward-McCann, New York, 1961), p. 188.
2. Fairfax Downey, *The Guns at Gettysburg* (David McKay Co. New York, 1958), p. 108.
3. Edwin Fishel, *The Secret War for the Union* (Houghton-Mifflin, Boston, 1996), p. 538.
4. Ibid.
5. Douglas S. Freeman, *Lee's Lieutenants* (Charles Schriber's Sons, New York, 1944), pp. 144–145.
6. Downey, op. cit.
7. Fishel, op. cit., p. 538.
8. *Just South of Gettysburg,* edited by F. Klein (The Newman Press, Westminster, Md., 1963), p. 164.
9. Ibid., p. 175.
10. Ibid. (map by Weldon).
11. Ibid., p. 160.

James Longstreet, *From Manassas to Appomattox* (Mallard Press, New York, 1991), p. 414.
12. "Then and Now," from M. Laswell's *Rags and Hope* (Coward-McCann, New York, 1961), Jacket.

Chapter Four

1. James Longstreet, *From Manassas to Appomattox* (Mallard Press, New York, 1991), p. 331.
2. Glenn Tucker, *Chickamauga* (Bobbs-Merril Co., New York, 1961), pp. 86–88.
3. Ibid., p. 92.
4. Ibid.
5. Ibid., pp. 92–93.
6. John Bowers, *Chickamauga and Chattanooga* (Harper Collins, New York, 1994), pp. 4–5.
7. Longstreet, op. cit., pp. 446–447.
8. Tucker, op. cit., p. 97.
9. Tucker, op. cit., pp. 97–98.
10. Longstreet, op. cit., p. 437.
11. Tucker, op. cit., p. 97.
12. Tucker, op. cit., pp. 97–98.

13. Longstreet, op. cit., p. 437.
14. Tucker, op. cit. P. 89.
15. Tucker, op. cit., p. 90.
16. Mary Laswell, *Rags and Hope* (Coward-McCann, New York, 1961), p. 187.
17. Tucker, op. cit.
18. Tucker, op. cit.
19. "Chickamauga and Chattanooga," National Park Service Pamphlet, (GPO 387-038 1995), p. 1.
20. John Bowers, *Chickamauga and Chattanooga* (Harper Collins, New York, 1994), p. 21.
21. Longstreet, op. cit., p. 439.
22. Tucker, op. cit., p. 262.
23. Tucker, op. cit., pp. 262–263.
24. Tucker, op. cit., p. 257.
25. Tucker, op. cit., p. 267.
26. Bowers, op. cit., pp. 120–121.
27. Bowers, op. cit., p. 125.
28. Bowers, op. cit., pp. 137–138.
29. Bowers, op. cit., pp. 157–158.
30. Longstreet, op. cit., p. 461.
31. Longstreet, op. cit., p. 462.
32. Longstreet, op. cit., pp. 465–468.
33. Longstreet, op. cit., p. 468.
34. Longstreet, op. cit., p. 469.
35. Longstreet, op. cit., p. 471.
36. Longstreet, op. cit.

Chapter Five

1. Mary Laswell, *Rags and Hope* (Coward McCann, New York, 1961), pp. 13–15.
2. John Bowers, *Chickamauga and Chattanooga* (Harper Collins, New York, 1994), p. 193–196.
3. Ibid., p. 193.
4. Laswell, op. cit., p. 216.
5. "Chattanooga," by Glenn Tucker, in *Civil War Times Illustrated* (Harrisburg, Pa., 1971), p. 20.
6. Laswell, op. cit., p. 217.
7. Laswell, op. cit.
8. Bowers, op. cit., p. 176.
9. Laswell, op. cit., pp. 218–220.

10. Laswell, op. cit., pp. 221–222.
11. Bowers, op. cit., p. 240.
12. Laswell, op. cit., pp. 236–238.
13. Laswell op. cit., pp. 239–240.
14. Laswell, op. cit., p. 242.
15. Laswell op. cit., p. 247.
16. Laswell, op. cit., p. 255.
17. Laswell, op. cit., p. 256.
18. Laswell, op. cit., p. 275.

Chapter Six

1. "Chattanooga," by Glenn Tucker in *Civil War Times Illustrated,* (Harrisburg, Pa, 1971), p. 19.
2. Ibid., p. 25.
3. Mary Laswell, *Rags and Hope* (Coward McCann, New York, 1961), p. 49.

Chapter Seven

1. James Longstreet, *From Manassas to Appomattox,* (Mallard Press, New York, 1941) in B & B, p. 274.
2. Nash Burger and J. Bettersworth, *South of Appomattox* (Harcourt Brace Co., New York, 1959), p. 276.
3. Ibid., p. 281.
4. Ibid., p. 282.
5. Ibid., p. 288.
6. Ibid.
7. Ibid., p. 292.
8. Ibid., p. 294.
9. Ibid., p. 296.
10. Mark Gerzon, *A House Divided,* (Putnam Sons, New York, 1997), p. xii.
11. Ibid.
12. "Being Civil May Save Democracy," *The Record,* May 28, 1998, p. A 5.
13. Ibid.
14. "New Civil War," by G. McGovern in *The Record,* January, 1998, p. A 10.

15. Burger and Bettersworth, op. cit., p. 300.
16. "Interest Groups Loud and Clear," *The Record,* March 8, 1998, p. A 9.
17. Ibid.
18. Ibid.
19. "Is There any Hope?" by E. J. Dionne Jr. *The Record,* March 1, 1998, p. 5.